HEALING

IT'S NOT WHAT YOU THINK . . .

Decoding the Mystery of Healing

MARCEL KLASEN

Dear Marilyn,

Enjoy this book

as an extension

of our healing connection.

May your life

be filled with

joy, love & blessings!

Aug. 12th, 2012   Marcel

ISBN-10: 146811168X
ISBN-13: 978-1468111682

WHAT PEOPLE SAY ABOUT MARCEL

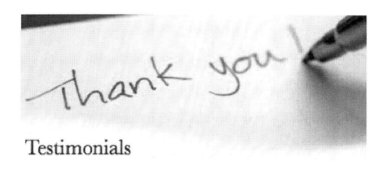

Testimonials

"The art of healing has always been an interest of mine but it wasn't until I met Marcel that I realized it needed to be a focus in my life. Marcel is a gifted teacher and healer. He has the ability through his creative gifts, to gently guide each individual to self-awareness and self-healing. He uses multiple modalities to create an atmosphere of trust allowing individuals to learn at their own pace, resulting in true understanding and empowerment. An extraordinary healer and a talented musician, this book is simply an extension of his gifts and will help guide and inspire healing to all who read it."

—Nancy J. DiNardo
Chairwoman of the Democratic State Central Committee

"Marcel is a very special healer who has touched my life and that of my family in a deeply moving way. Even though I was skeptical at first, Marcel helped me to rapidly overcome a personal challenge that affected my work and my personal life. He is one of those rare people who can help you heal and be free from emotional obstructions."

—Lorenzo Minoli
Emmy® Award-winning Movie Producer
Producer/Author of *Have No Fear: The Life of John Paul II*

"In this book leading energy healer Marcel truly removes the *mystery* surrounding the timeless, ancient and present practice of energy healing as yet another of his gifts to the world. Information that is this powerful and effective should be required reading. Thank you Marcel for all you do."

—Tom Nicoli
Award-winning Hypnotherapist
Author of *Thinking Thin* and *A Better You by Hypnosis*

"Marcel's book on healing the body, mind and spirit delightfully explains the mysterious secrets he has learned on his path to become a masterful teacher and healer. His clients' testimonials reveal his gifts."

—Dick Sutphen
Bestselling Author of *You Were Born Again to Be Together* and *Soul Agreements*

"Marcel is a diamond in the rough. A best-kept secret that shouldn't be a secret. He has helped me and other people with his relaxed and easy approach. No judgment, no pressure. Marcel is very intuitive and aware and he knows more about me than I do myself at times. It is good to trust in someone who shares love and promotes healing the way he does and who knows how to combine it with his vast knowledge to help you improve your life."

—Matt Criscuolo
Jazz Musician/Composer

"When I met Marcel I needed help. A number of issues were clouding my mind and were impeding me to think and act. Fear and panic were dominating my life. I was very skeptical at first, but my life and my behavior changed overnight! The subsequent healing sessions with Marcel were not the search for the solution, but the solution itself. Marcel helped me find it within myself in only three weeks. I started to become the person that I wanted to be not the person I was. My wife still can't believe what has happened. I continue to explore myself realizing the value of Marcel's healing work everyday."

—Marino Marin
Investment Banker

"Marcel has a gift for helping children overcome their difficulties. My nine year old has many anxieties. Marcel was able to help in a way that was both fun and appealing to him. My son was able to learn from Marcel in a gentle, relaxed and even in a musical way. This allowed him to understand his personal challenges and celebrate his strengths at the same time. I have tried various approaches with my son but Marcel was able to reach a level of healing with him that no one else was able to do!"

—Lisa Gold
Mother of Sam and Alex

"Marcel has been a tremendous help in significantly reducing the effects of my diabetes mellitus. Frozen shoulders, back pain, foot malformation, numbness and overall circulation have all drastically improved. My blood sugar usually stabilizes for quite some time after a session with Marcel. His healing work has stopped my recurrent eye hemorrhages. I was gradually becoming blind but my vision has improved and I can now continue doing my artwork. I am so happy to have found Marcel to help with all the complications of my condition."

—Juliet Kirby
Botanical Artist

"I have observed Marcel's growth in experience and wisdom as a teacher and instructor over the past twenty years. I am so glad now to see he has expanded his outreach with his informative new book."

—Dr. Dwight F. Damon
President of the National Guild of Hypnotists

"I am very thankful to Marcel for all his healing support for my family. He has helped us in so many ways. From hypnosis for childbirth, nail biting, back pain and attention issues to hormonal imbalances and emotional challenges. We are so thrilled that Marcel has been a part of our lives for the past ten years, and we look forward to many happy and healthy years with his help."

—Lisa Kapnick
Mother of Jake and Zachary

"Following my diagnosis with breast cancer, Marcel helped me stay calm and optimistic as I underwent various treatments and maintained a substantial job. Marcel helped me create my own healing tools so I can visualize and meditate to relax, create positive energy, and limit stress. The insights Marcel has given me I will use for the rest of my life."

—Sue Oddie
Bank Executive

"On behalf of the children, families and staff at Schneider Children's Hospital, we wish to thank Marcel for the wonderful performance he put on for the children during the holiday season. His thoughtfulness and talents gave joy and diversion during their hospitalization. Many of our children face chronic, long-term, and often life-threatening illnesses. Marcel's happy songs are outstanding and the children really benefited from his healing music."

—Glenn Schifano
Music Therapist/Child Life Specialist

"For many years Marcel has helped my family and me with his unique healing abilities. His extraordinary work has contributed to our health in many ways."

—Michael Vranos and Family
Hedge Fund Manager, Philanthropist

"Marcel offers what is unique in a book on energy healing … he adds heart. The art and science of healing embraces not only what you know but how you share what you know. I have observed Marcel working with clients and he has worked on me. He is both gentle and powerful in his deep understanding of the healing arts. He has heart in working with people, whether intuiting the source of a problem or playing his wonderfully healing music. Marcel is a much-loved member of our Stillpoint Community and has shown himself to be a true healer in every sense of the word. Congratulations on this meaningful new book."

—Meredith Young-Sowers, D.Div
Founder/Director of the Stillpoint School of Integrative Life Healing
Author of *Agartha*, *Wisdom Bowls*, *Angelic Messenger Cards*, and *Spirit Heals*

This book is dedicated to my special mentor
and best friend Dr. Sonja de Graaff van Mastrigt.
Her inspiration, motivation, and medical intuition
have enabled me to move beyond my perceived limitations
and to grow into the healer that I am today.

~ Marcel

Contents

PREFACE

When I was first introduced to Marcel in 1981, it was immediately clear to me that he would make a powerful difference in the lives of many people. Not only does one quickly feel calm in the presence of Marcel's healing energy, his compassion for those in need and his willingness to help people make him unlike anyone I have ever known. His powerful healing energy restores the body and mind back to balance and enables deep healing to begin.

Marcel is one of the kindest and most giving men I know. His gentle voice and musical compositions create a world of tranquility and peacefulness. In that state we rest and heal. I feel privileged to have been working together with this gifted healer for more than twenty-five years. During this time, as a physician, I have witnessed many miraculous healings in patients and I have seen how Marcel's work has dramatically improved the health of many people, producing measurable results, physically, emotionally, and mentally. The lives of patients, friends, and family members were touched forever in a positive way.

On a personal note, Marcel has guided me safely with his healing gift through breast cancer. I owe much gratitude for healing to Marcel and the miracle of a second chance for my life. His gift is amazing and multi-faceted. It helps the body and mind to activate its highest healing potential. Moreover, Marcel's light awakens happiness and contentment. Maybe once in a lifetime one meets a special human being whose life is devoted to benefit humankind with compassion and healing. Marcel has taught me much about consistent kindness, compassion, healing, and selfless devotion. Just like mine, many lives have been touched and changed in a positive way by Marcel. He brings healing and light to those in need. Many of us thank him for the gift of healing on the brink of death.

Healing, It's Not What You Think . . . will inspire you to your own path of healing. Marcel's work is a revelation to all who are desperately searching for solutions to the challenges they feel in their lives. The essence of this book is about the powerful healing force that is present in our own body and mind. Marcel shares with us his insights and practical tools to awaken and support this innate healing force. You hold in your hands the key to unlocking your true healing potential. You can begin your own journey to health and happiness. I hope you will benefit as much as I have from Marcel's wisdom and gift of healing.

Dr. Sonja de Graaff
Personal Physician

Introduction

"Healing is a matter of time,
but it is sometimes also a matter of opportunity."

~ Hippocrates

This book has a central theme: *Decoding the Mystery of Healing.* This main subject branches out in three sub-themes throughout the book. *An Insider's Look into the Life of a Healer* is one. *The Role of the Mind in Healing* is another. *Translating the Complexity of Healing into Simple Methods* is number three. These topics all provide opportunities that can raise your awareness about healing. Applying them can cause extraordinary healing effects on your body, mind, and spirit. These opportunities are brought to you in the form of stories, descriptions, and techniques with tremendous healing potential for all human beings, for all animals, and for all of planet Earth.

If one part of you finds this intriguing while another part says "Yes, but—", keep on reading. The *but* part may soon fade as the awareness sets in that you already know quite a few things about healing from personal experience. Chances are that your life has been full of examples of positive energy shifts. You might have been uncertain about your role in the healing process of these events, but that may just be the reason you picked up this book.

Wouldn't it be great if you knew how to positively influence your life and accelerate healing? Well, you are about to discover how you can make this happen. Through connecting with my gifts and the special methods I have developed, you will be able to tap into new applications for your individual path and move onward and upward in life. No matter how great the challenges, you have the capacity to use your mind to redirect the energy around any situation that affects you or people you feel connected to.

Positive Change Happens

Without a doubt, our world is changing and things are not the way they used to be. To many of us it feels as if our life in this world is changing so quickly that we cannot keep up with it. Whether we like it or not, change happens but we want it to occur in moderation and we hope for change we can choose. We like positive change especially if we are in control of it. As the saying goes, "If you don't create change, change will create you." Many of us spend lots of time and energy trying to influence others to make happy change happen but we often overlook that real change comes from within. We are willing to allow change as long as it connects with our beliefs, our personal truth. That truth itself can also be changed and many of us wish we could do this quickly. However, the same mind mechanism that helps us to create our belief systems seems to prevent us from undoing them if they do not work for us anymore.

For more than twenty-five years I have been working with thousands of people who have chosen me to be the facilitator for the life changes they desire. Some came to me with physical problems, others were in emotional pain, and then there were many people looking for more spiritual meaning in their life. As amazing results and extraordinary healings occurred, I became more and more fascinated with this mysterious energy. When I learned to trust my own gift and to believe in my ability to help others create positive changes, I was ready to accept my identity and responsibilities as a healer. Over time, I have developed my own unique methods and techniques that work effectively and efficiently to help improve people's quality of life. In this book I share my experiences and insights with you.

The Pursuit of Healing

Since childhood I have studied and practiced modalities that use positive energy to favorably influence people's quality of life. I discovered there is a mysterious healing force that provides people, animals, and all other organisms with life-sustaining power. It can also balance existing energies to create harmony and vitality. Known as *prana* by the Hindus, *chi* by the Chinese, and *ki* by the Japanese, it is widely accepted as an important source of health and wellbeing in more than ninety cultures around the world. In Western culture it is often referred to as the *healing force*.

Present-day technology, bio-energy frequency scanning devices, and energy imagery equipment such as Kirlian photography enable us to observe and record energy as it moves and blocks, shifts and stagnates, and affects the world around us and within us. All humans have the possibility to tap into this source and many have been at the receiving end of it without conscious awareness. Some of us have a naturally high sensitivity to energy fluctuations. They are often negatively influenced, feel drained, or become ill.

As a child I had an extraordinary experience that made me decide to fully explore my natural ability to perceive, interpret, and apply this healing energy. As I grew up, I became determined to learn how to improve my skills to help people heal and create the life they desire. Over the years, I have developed a unique combination of various energy-healing modalities linked with the power of the mind. My ability to detect and adjust imbalances in someone's energy system is linked with the potential of that person's mind to move into a brainwave state known as trance. In this state of mind I can use specific suggestions to amplify the effectiveness of that person's own healing force. In essence, this method boosts the process of healing and self-improvement, and speeds up positive change. When I work in someone's energy field, with what is known as high vibrational frequencies, healing is super-accelerated.

Since I introduced this new concept into my practice, the results my clients have had are amazing. It works better and faster than using energy-healing modalities or hypnosis separately. All components—physical, emotional, mental, and spiritual—are addressed simultaneously to create new pathways for healing. The aim of these sessions is to make a unique energy adjustment. This subtle modification has far-reaching and long-lasting positive effects on a person. In a hypnotic trance the human mind has the capacity to perceive vibrational frequencies that go beyond conscious, three-dimensional awareness. It is in these realms that deep healing and instantaneous transformations occur.

It's Not What You Think

As the title of this book suggests, when it comes to finding healing and establishing a long-lasting positive shift, it's not what you *think*. The thinking, or conscious part of our mind, is limited and often incorrect. Our individual truth is mostly based on our emotions and subconscious programs. To heal the past, enjoy the present, and feel enthusiastic about the future, it's not simply what we *think* that will make a difference. Permanent change begins as soon as we take our initial thought pattern to another level of awareness where we *feel* different about ourselves and truly believe it.

This book describes the components of my special healing approach and it explains its process. Personal anecdotes, case histories, and other stories will illustrate the importance of developing conscious awareness of one's mind. Furthermore, it aims to expand the possibilities to influence, upgrade, or reprogram our inner autopilot, the subconscious mind.

Chapter one tells you about the life-changing transitions I went through while growing up that laid the foundation for my work as a healer. Through a number of extraordinary personal experiences, I elaborate on the nature of *energy* and how positive and negative feelings have had a profound effect on the way I have learned to think and feel.

Chapter two gives an explanation of *hypnosis*, how the human mind operates, and how the differences between the conscious and subconscious parts influence our behavior. This part of the book will help to you to better understand why thinking about change will, in itself, not produce the desired result and why hypnosis is such a fast-acting modality to really achieve your goals.

Chapter three describes the *subtle energy system* known as *the aura* and *the chakras*. This subtle system is extremely useful for self-actualization and for your ability to communicate with other people about any personal challenge. Illustrations and charts give clarity to the complexity of these ancient frames of reference and help define your physical, emotional, and spiritual ups and downs.

Chapter four shows how to enhance your intuitive perception and accurately read people's energy through my five-step *BLESS method*. It is an invaluable tool for anyone interested in the promotion of healing. This five-step approach explains how to detect energy fluctuations and how to efficiently produce a scan of a person's energy using only your hands and your mind.

Chapter five introduces my unique method called *Positive Mind Mapping*, an effective and intuitive way for both children and adults to better focus their mind. This approach supports academics, athletics, and creative expression. It serves as an aid to study and organize information, solve problems, and make decisions. Positive mind mapping also helps to improve memory, focus attention, and stimulate motivation. This method is an excellent tool for kids with ADHD and adults with concentration and/or learning problems.

Chapter six is all about *music* and how *sound vibrations* affect us. Music is a potent tool for restoring the inner harmony of the body and awakening the spirit. Understanding how and why the energy of sound and music affects us, without any thought involved, is essential for healing. Applying the musical principles of entrainment, resonance, toning, and harmonics can help us achieve overall wellness, greater vitality, and a deep level of fulfillment.

Chapter seven explains how *instant energy healing* works and how anyone can learn how to do this. There will be a description of my specific technique, called *the AHA method*, designed to create a happy mind in just seven seconds. It is a fascinating and easy-to-learn self-help tool that a growing number of people around the world are applying to experience the three Cs of personal healing power— *calmness, clarity, confidence.*

Happy Number Seven

The number *seven* kept announcing itself to me whenever I needed to make a method more practical or to simplify some complex information. I realized that seven is a very useful number for clarity and organization. There are seven days in a week, seven colors of the rainbow, seven different notes in a regular musical scale, seven major chakras, seven auras, seven seas and Seven Wonders of the World. The word *healing* is composed of seven letters, and did you know that science regards seven as a *happy number*? Yes indeed, mathematics actually distinguishes it as such.

The symbolic and subliminal power of seven can certainly not be ignored. It is regarded by every major religion as a *sacred number*. In feng shui, the Oriental art of placement, seven is the number of a perfectly completed cycle. In numerology, seven represents truth and the accumulation of knowledge and wisdom. It is, therefore, no coincidence that this book has seven chapters while I am in my forty-ninth year on planet Earth— seven times seven.

If you are new to the world of healing you may enjoy this book for its uncomplicated descriptions while gaining more knowledge on the infinite potential of the human mind. If you are more advanced on this subject, this book may help you to look at it from a different point of view and further deepen your knowledge and skills. You can apply the special techniques and new methods either for your own journey or to help other people improve their lives. As a healer, my greatest fulfillment has always been to support people into self-empowerment. It brings joy and meaning to my life to serve as a healing guide or life coach for other people's process of positive change. I hope this book will open your mind to new pathways for healing and happiness. Just imagine the possibilities!

Chapter 1

THE MYSTERY OF HEALING

"The art of healing comes from nature, not from the physician.
Therefore the physician must start from nature, with an open mind."

~ Paracelsus

Healing Secrets

How many times in your life did you need healing? Most likely, countless times. From the time you were a newborn baby to your present age you have gone through many levels of healing. You may have had a simple skin rash that came and went, or your healing may have been a continuing story with ongoing episodes. It is fascinating to hear people describe their most significant healing stories because they are usually not only about physical healing. This book will give you examples of healing stories that may be very similar to what you are hoping to find in your life. As a result, you may be able to speed up your own healing process. There are so many different aspects to your wellbeing and, therefore, so many different ways to heal. Healing is a complex subject, and it can be a spontaneous event or a structured approach. Depending upon the various meanings of the word, it can range from personal, physical relief to spiritual enlightenment of the entire planet.

In my work as a healer I have been blessed with the ability to guide healing energy efficiently and to help speed up other people's healing. Some came to me with chronic conditions, others with acute problems looking for additional help in their healing process. Some were in distress, others felt stuck and without purpose. A lot of my clients were suddenly hit with a life-threatening diagnosis such as cancer and confronted with the notion that their life might soon be over. But healing is always possible and it is my greatest fulfillment to know that many of these people are now free from their problem or disease and are living a joyful life.

So how exactly does this mysterious healing force happen? Is there a specific scientific explanation for it or is it mostly a mystical experience? How can you promote your own healing or that of your loved ones and what modalities are applicable to your personal challenges? The descriptions, methods, and stories in this book aim to help you find answers to these questions and decode the *mystery of healing* in a simplified manner. The word *healing* is linguistically related to the word *wholing*, which describes something fragmented becoming complete again. A healer's skills to help fit the pieces of the healing together make him a valuable contributor to other people's health and wellbeing. My own healing path started when I was a young boy who needed to fit the pieces of his own puzzle together. I learned some important secrets about healing early in my life and I would like to share them with you.

Expression versus Suppression

I love people, I always have. From day one, I have been particularly fascinated with people's voices. I learned to talk before I could walk and communicating with other people became an ongoing activity as I grew older. My parents often told me that, as a baby, I was already fixated on anything that could produce sounds and I particularly seemed to enjoy listening to the sound of conversations. It must have been adorable and funny to watch a one-year-old intently following a dialogue between people, looking as if I knew what they were talking about. The little boy Marcel soon became known as a *good listener*, a positive label I have tried to live up to ever since.

Early on in life, I also showed a strong connection to music. As a toddler, no radio, record player, or musical instrument escaped my attention. When I got my hands on a harmonica, I was soon playing actual tunes with our dog, Teddy, howling along. I developed a craving for sounds and music, and when satisfied, I was a happy humdinger singing along with songs on the radio that caught my ear. In an unhappy mood, when frustrated or when otherwise challenged, I could annoyingly scream at the top of my lungs. I had a need to express myself through the energy of sound, but often the receivers and bystanders did not appreciate the effort. In energy terms, our frequencies did not always resonate.

At age seven, my schoolteacher, Ms. Steenwijk, dismissed me from the classroom because I was disruptive. I was humming along to the music in my mind, but a little too much and a little too loud. I obviously misinterpreted her reprimanding words when she yelled, "Marcel, get out . . . out . . . out!" Instead of waiting in the hallway, I went *out* the classroom door, *out* the door into the schoolyard, *out* the gate, and then all the way home. You can imagine my mother's surprise to see me come home at such an unusual time and she thought I might have gotten sick. I said, "No Mom, it's not what you think." When I told her I was sent home for "making music" she put on her coat and immediately took me back to school to have a serious talk with the teacher and the principal.

As it turned out, Ms. Steenwijk had no idea that I had left the building and when everything was explained, suddenly everybody started laughing and it seemed best for me to join them. Though it wasn't really her fault, my teacher felt bad about the situation and decided to buy me a genuine Hohner harmonica that I was to play only at special occasions like birthdays and other celebrations. From that time on, I was acknowledged as the official *class musician* to be called to duty for any celebration or ceremony. I was really excited about this and not just because my new function gave me a chance to stand out. Young as I was, this helped me to better understand the responsibility of keeping my *sound energy* under control.

Understanding is one thing, putting your knowledge into practice is another thing. Especially in a sensitive, imaginative, and often-hyperactive child, this type of creative energy could only be suppressed to a certain extent. I now had to observe the world without processing my thoughts and feelings in a natural way. This created more and more tension inside.

Also at the age of seven, I had my first and, to this day, only surgical procedure, a tonsillectomy. I remember it as a horrible event worsened by the sight of my mother fainting in the recovery room after watching me continuously cough up blood. My throat took a very long time to heal. It is very well possible that I exaggerated the pain to get my daily fix of ice cream. This commonly accepted and doctor-approved post-tonsillectomy remedy really helped to soothe the suffering. On the other hand, it also compounded the message *when in pain, eat ice cream*. As I will describe in chapter two, this is a way in which a child's mind is programmed for comfort food patterns that may lead to out-of-control cravings, and even eating disorders in adults.

Despite the delicious remedy, over the next few years the combination of vocal suppression, throat trauma, and voice abuse resulted in the sound of my voice becoming constrained and often hoarse. I became more and more anxious and hyperactive and even started having nightmares. Then, when I was eleven-years-old, I lost my voice completely. It happened in the early morning hours after waking up from a very scary dream. The event and its aftermath indicated a turning point in my young life and I remember it in great detail.

Voice Trauma

This was not an ordinary nightmare; it was a recurring, very frightening dream that seemed to come in cycles and was always around the same theme—a hooded man without a face coming to get me. The scariest part was that while in the dream, I knew what was happening and what would come next. Lying in bed, I knew that the door to my bedroom was open. A mix of worried thoughts and anxious feelings would go through my mind. *"The door was supposed to be closed! Didn't I close it? Did I forget to check it before I went to sleep? I'm sure it was closed, who left it open? My brothers? My parents? Where are they anyway? Whose footsteps do I hear on the stairs? Oh no . . . it's that man again. Oh no . . . I can't move! I have to call for help . . . but then he will hear me. I'm scared!"*

On those nights I would wake myself up and after a brief moment of literally feeling petrified, I was then able to breathe out, relax, and loosen up. I would switch on my bedside lamp to realize that it was just

THE MYSTERY OF HEALING

the same dream again, the scary one that I had had so many times before. Not this time. I felt like my dream had me in its grip and the suspense was building. The hooded man was now standing in the doorway of my bedroom towering over me, waiting, as if he was contemplating his next move. I felt totally helpless and there was no way to escape. I thought, *this is the end.* Convinced that he would now snatch me, zap me, or do something else of a horrible nature that scary, hooded people are known to do, I struggled in a last attempt to free myself. I opened my mouth as wide as possible to let out the loudest scream I could produce.

Then, silence and darkness. I felt my heart beating in my throat, a strange feeling. No movement, eyes still closed. *Don't breathe, Marcel,* I heard an inner voice saying, *not a sound.* My mouth was open and felt dry. The voice whispered, *don't swallow, not a sound.* I must have been lying in that catatonic state for at least ten minutes. Then, my younger brother who I shared the bedroom with switched on the light to go to the bathroom. That seemed to bring me back to reality, but when I tried to say a few words to him there was no sound in my voice, just a whispering noise— very odd. I tried to go back to sleep, but after this horrifying experience, I decided it was safer to stay awake and wait for the sun to rise.

My voice had not returned by daybreak. I succeeded in hiding this from my three brothers, which seemed to be the best strategy. After all, not being able to speak immediately puts you in the "dumb" category and who wants that? Of course, my mother could not be fooled. I was not exactly a silent kid, rather the opposite, so she immediately noticed something was wrong and she joked, "Am I going deaf or have you lost your voice?" Initially, she must have assumed that this was just another one of Marcel's acts to get attention and after checking my temperature, she concluded that my inconvenience should clear up before the end of the day. Armed with a bag of cough drops, I went to school.

Not being able to use verbal communication may have been a blessing for the teacher but it was pure agony for me. What's more, there did not seem to be any improvement by lunchtime and at the end of the day I was still voiceless. Playing the optimist, I wrote to my schoolmates on a pad, "Sorry guys, I lost my voice. I'm sure it's out there somewhere. There is a reward for whoever finds it first!" Back home at the dinner table, my father thought I was exaggerating and my two older brothers thought it was a game, so they tried to trick me into speech. When that didn't work, they tickled and tackled me, but still, no sound.

When my voice had not returned the next day, my mom became worried and brought me to an ear, nose, and throat specialist. With his headband magnifier on and his tongue depressor in my mouth, the doctor took his time looking at my throat. "Say aah," he said. I tried, but all I could produce was a gurgling sound. "Mmm", the doctor said. I became uncomfortable and I started to gag. Then he called my mother over to have a look while pointing out white spots and inflammation. The same voice that came in my head after my nightmare started to whisper to me again, *Don't breathe, Marcel . . . not a sound*. At that point, the doctor, while still in my face, held my tongue down with his spatula and called the nurse over to also take a peek. I started to see stars and then I fainted. When I came to, the doctor was holding my head down. "Feeling better now?" he asked. I had only been out for a brief moment and I felt lightheaded. "I'm sorry," he said. Didn't expect you to be that sensitive."

He diagnosed me with vocal nodules. These callous spots on my vocal chords had caused the symptoms I experienced. To get rid of the nodules, surgery was an option, but that could create scar tissue and possibly more problems down the line. The doctor recommended for me to first see a speech pathologist and work on the cause of the issue. Research evidence suggested that these kind of physical problems were the result of stress and anxiety. In other words, I had to stop being a vocal over doer and use my voice more wisely by learning how to relax.

Voice Healing

Over the next few days, my voice came back somewhat but speaking normally continued to take a lot of energy out of me. I went to see Miss Mooi. Her Dutch last name translates into English as *beautiful*. I remember my first appointment with her very well. With her long blond hair, her smiling face, and her soothing voice, I instantly had a crush on her. "This could be good," I thought. As it turned out, I was right about that, in more ways than I could have imagined at the time.

Rather than teaching me how to use my voice better, Miss Mooi first taught me how to breathe properly. She told me to lie down on a treatment table to place one hand on my belly and one on my chest. Then, I had to take slow, deep breaths and make sure that the lower hand moved up while the upper hand stayed down. It seemed fairly simple, but it went against what felt normal to me so I did not automatically get it right that first time. However, I was determined to impress Miss Mooi and I promised her I would practice every day until I saw her again the next week. And I did. It was easiest for me to practice at night while I was in bed getting ready to go to sleep.

On my next session, I showed off my new skill and Miss Mooi was indeed impressed. "Now, let's take it step further," she said." While I demonstrated my breathing exercise with my eyes closed, I heard her calming voice talking to me as if she was telling a story. She said, "Imagine now, you are lying on a beach . . . and it's summertime . . . and the sun is shining brightly . . . and you start to feel more and more comfortable ... and you feel your body becoming nice and warm . . . and you can almost hear the sound of ocean waves rolling in and out in the same way as you are breathing."

And the story went on with me having a great time, enjoying myself in this wonderful vacation place. Miss Mooi gave me an open ending so that I could continue the story on my own. And so I practiced daily to go to my happy vacation place. Later in life, I learned that she was using a form of hypnosis on me called guided imagery.

The next week Miss Mooi told me to *let the sunlight melt away the white spots on my vocal chords.* Because I trusted her completely, I took her suggestions literally and the fact that I secretly was in love with her made me even more susceptible to her words. The relaxation and self-suggestion techniques she taught me worked amazingly well and my voice was healing rapidly!

The vocal nodules disappeared in a few weeks, my voice became calmer and fuller, and I could now talk and sing louder without losing my voice or my energy. On top of that, over a period of four months Miss Mooi also taught me self-help methods to positively influence whatever it was that bothered me. Being a sensitive and rather hyperactive child, I was prone to having headaches, sleep problems, and nausea. All of this began to change as I was learning how to use the power of my own mind.

The Breath of Life Exercise

1. Find a place where you can sit or lie down quietly in a comfortable position.
2. Gently close your eyes completely.
3. Place one hand on your belly and one on your chest.
4. Take a deep breath and let the lower hand go up while the upper hand stays down.
5. Continue taking long, deep breaths, while repeating this phrase in your mind, *Breathing in, I calm my body and mind. Breathing out, I smile.*
6. After a few minutes, count from seven to one and then open your eyes.
7. Take one more deep breath of life and say, *I feel good.*

Initiation

Interestingly, I found out that I could now decide what I wanted to dream about at night. All I needed to do was the quick relaxation technique just before I went to sleep while repeating some words relating to the mind movie I wanted to experience. One night, I felt the courage to actually choose to let my recurring horrifying dream appear once more and my goal was to be fully prepared to vanquish the hooded man. It worked like a charm but in a way I never expected.

Certainly, the dream appeared with all its familiar features—the open door to my bedroom, the sounds of footsteps on the staircase, his dark appearance. Something was very different though. I was neither anxious nor angry. In fact, I felt kind of sorry for the guy as he stood in the doorway. I told him, "Why don't you take off your hood, so I can see what you look like?" When he revealed himself, there was no face or a real body, only something that looked like a colorful light that seemed to flow like liquid and barely touched the ground. "Are you a ghost?" I asked. I did not get an answer but when I reached out to touch this light energy, I felt an incredible, happy feeling inside.

Then, the light turned into a mirror image of my own face, glowing and smiling in a caring way. No words were exchanged, but I remember feeling my heartbeat and then an echo as if there was a transmission and a reception. My breath was calm and steady, my mind was clear and at peace. The image faded and I drifted into a sound and restful sleep.

When I woke up, I felt at ease and an inner smile gently pulsated through my body. I knew that something very important had occurred in my extraordinary dream experience. At the age of eleven, I could not yet foresee the extent of it, but later in life I realized that this event symbolized my initiation as a healer. The memory of this dream is vividly etched in my subconscious mind. From that point forward, I approached life differently, feeling a connection with this light being, having frequent conversations with it, and receiving guidance as I was trying to find my place and purpose in the world.

Intuitive Healing

After this extraordinary experience, I began to look at life from a different point of view. The recurring nightmares stopped and I began to *sense* things beyond my normal range of perception. Initially it appeared to always involve emotionally upset people. I felt an energetic attraction to people who were either angry or sad or fearful. I often chose friends who did not have the same kind of stability and happiness at home as I did. When board games became boring, I usually ended up being the *good listener* that I was labeled to be ten years earlier while my buddy got his troubles off his chest and felt much better afterward.

I also discovered that if I gently placed my hands on someone's shoulders or head, it had a calming effect on them and it changed their mood almost immediately. I tried to show people how to do this but the effect seemed to be a lot weaker when they did the same thing. Intuitively, I started using healing touch more and more when someone I met was not feeling well. It only took a few moments of *energy healing* while applying the breath of life exercise. I imagined breathing in what was bothering the other person and then blowing it out again into the space around me.

The father of one of my friends, Mr. Simon, had a chronic sleeping disorder but always slept like a baby each time after I had stopped by. I was not very confident yet about my healing gift but I remember Mr. Simon calling me an angel and he even seriously asked my parents if I could come to live in his house. A nice thing to hear, but I liked my own family enough to decline the offer.

One of our neighbors, Mrs. De Koning, was an elderly widow with a respiratory disease and she used an oxygen tank to help her breathe. I sometimes mowed her lawn or went to get her groceries. She really enjoyed me coming over to tell stories and jokes that made her laugh out loud. In those moments there was no sign of breathing difficulty, no look of distress in her eyes, no muscle spasms. My mom said that she was very lonely after her husband passed away, which was probably the main source of her suffering. My ability to connect with healing energy may have neutralized the symptoms enough to help her feel alive and well again for a while.

Alex, a six-year-old boy across the street, had cancer and went through chemotherapy. His hair loss was scary to most kids and they avoided contact with him. To me, it felt natural and normal to spend time with him playing chess and card games. We also had simple fun singing along with records and recording silly jingles on a cassette recording. Against the odds he survived his disease and his mother told me she believed it was the fun and games that helped it happen. At the time I may not have been sure about that, but now I certainly believe that joy is a very powerful healing component. It may well have saved Alex's life.

Music

Also at age eleven, my love for music convinced my parents to buy me a brand-new Yamaha classical guitar. It was a beautiful instrument, shiny enough to see my reflection in the dark-colored wooden back. It came with fresh bronze and nylon strings and a special cloth to keep it clean. I remember wiping the dust and fingerprints off the varnished spruce top several times a day and I enjoyed smelling the distinct aroma of the wood. As I went to my weekly music lessons, my guitar and I became inseparable buddies. Secretly, I had conversations in my room with my guitar about the meaning of music in life and how we must create harmony together. It was already clear to my family that I was into music from birth. No musical instrument or anything that produced sound was left untouched by me, but this guitar was more than just a musical toy. To me, it became a doorway into a different world, a vehicle to go where other people cannot easily go. It connected me with that colorful light being in my dream and it helped me to feel inspired.

Even though I was rather lazy student when it came to practicing classical music, I did play a lot of pop music. I imitated songs from the radio or records and, just like my idol Paul McCartney, was playing by ear. This felt a lot more natural than translating sheet music into songs. My hands felt the strings of my guitar and instantly, off I went into a daydream state. I only took lessons for a few years, enough to develop some skills in reading musical notation. As time went by I became more proficient in playing music and even started composing my own songs. The original ability to link myself to a source outside my own capacity got stronger and stronger and it became an important component of the foundation of my healing practice, particularly when working with sound and vibrations.

Natural Energy

My teenage years were characterized by a search for independence. Being out on my own exploring the world around me was a favorite thing to do. This must have worried my parents at times, but I am grateful they gave me the freedom to experience life in my own way. With my love for nature I frequently wandered off into woods, through fields, over hills, along streams, near lakes, and toward the beach. Though I liked being around people, I had a strong desire to feel the freedom of a natural surrounding. It helped me feel relaxed and I always felt better after a walk in nature. I now understand that my inborn sensitivity to energy needed to be released and recharged to stay healthy and balanced.

All these experiences were stored in the archives of my subconscious, and in my sessions with clients I often use these natural images. During my walks and bike rides through nature I usually had conversations with an imaginary older, wiser, more mature version of me who already knew what life had in store for me. In my hypnosis training, I later learned to use this as a technique called *progression*, in which we look at the future full of optimism and enthusiasm to give our mind a positive direction.

Maturity

Maturity is known to come in seven-year cycles and I went through a new awareness phase at age seven. Around the age of fourteen, I felt another transition that was both exciting and confusing at times. My family and I moved to a new home and I went to a new high school with new schoolmates and new opportunities. Playtime seemed to be over and *work* became the keyword for the next five years. Schoolwork, in particular, was a new challenge for Marcel, the teenager who until now, had relied on his IQ, his intuition, and his ability to listen to do fairly well at school. This new situation was changing my life and required more discipline, more focused attention, and more motivation. During this life phase I found out that if I really wanted to have or achieve something, I had to make an effort. This applied to academics, athletics, creativity, social situations, and even making some money. Through trial and error I came to three important realizations about work:

1. Procrastination leads to frustration.
2. It's easier to do anything if you imagine you like it.
3. Work gets done more efficiently if you create routines.

It was also in this time of my life that my mind inevitably tried to make sense of gender differences. While still feeling uncertain, I reached these basic conclusions:

1. Boys and girls have different operating mechanisms.
2. Everybody wants to feel good.
3. Everyone likes music.

To form connections and friendships in this time, full of insecurity and mixed emotions, it seemed to make sense to pursue my path of healing through music. At age fifteen, I wrote my first song and a year later I performed at a school party with my first band and my first electrical guitar. Using amplifiers for my voice and my guitar created an awesome powerful feeling. I use this imagery often as a metaphor to explain my healing work: *Imagine being plugged in to an amplification device that jumpstarts a feeling of empowerment.*

After graduating high school I went to college and regained a sense of freedom. I also enjoyed performing as lead singer/guitarist of my new band. It was great to use the energy of celebration to connect with an audience through music. At the same time, I was able to use my voice to express myself creatively with the songs I had written. I felt spirited, independent, and ready to move further but did not yet know how to do so. Subconsciously, I knew I needed a guide, someone to help me make sense of it all and give direction to my life.

Connection

You may have heard this phrase before: *When the student is ready, the teacher will appear.* That saying certainly applied to me at the age of nineteen. With perfect timing I was introduced to Dr. Sonja, an enthusiastic and vibrant young physician specializing in integrative medicine. I signed up for her health and nutrition program and she shared much of her wisdom with me. Her guidance taught me how to optimize my energy and overall wellbeing in the most natural way. In the process, I became a firm believer in preventative medicine and conscious living. Blessed with the gift of medical intuition, Dr. Sonja also awakened my interest in spirituality and energy healing. She recognized my gifts and motivated me to take advanced training to be able to help people efficiently in their healing process. I followed her advice and I went to study and practice a wide range of healing modalities around the world.

In Europe, I served as a medic in the Royal Dutch Army Medical Corps, where I was thoroughly trained in human anatomy, physiology, and received my Red Cross diploma in combat emergency care. After that, I studied bodywork and reflexology and I became licensed in therapeutic massage. In Asia, I learned forms of oriental healing art such as acupressure, reiki healing, and feng shui. In The South Pacific I deepened my knowledge of polarity therapy as well as traditional shamanic approaches to healing. In the United States, intrigued with the power of the mind, I studied for over a decade with master hypnotists to eventually become a board-certified hypnosis expert myself.

I also obtained a master certification in advanced energy healing from the Stillpoint Institute, which has strengthened the spiritual connection of my work. I consider this last component to be the glue that keeps all healing modalities together. In my presentations I always emphasize this aspect of healing: the healing force must come *through* you, not *from* you. Without a connection to a higher source, a healer will become drained, depleted, and eventually ill. The principle of *healer heal thyself* has been an important value for me for many years as my healing work reminds me on a daily basis to practice what I teach. It is not complicated, just a matter of building routines. The breath of life exercise is a good example of this; I start and end each day with this routine. It helps me to be ready for a new day in the morning and to prepare for a good night's rest at bedtime. I intend to do this for the rest of my life because it keeps my thoughts, my feelings, and my actions in balance.

In my morning meditation I let all the people come to mind that I plan to meet that day and send them a good dose of positive energy in advance. Bright light is usually my vehicle of choice but sometimes, specific words, colors, or sounds feel more appropriate to use. I also imagine any people that are in need of extra care, help, or support to receive a strong amount of *compassion energy*. The whole process takes anywhere from five to ten minutes and I routinely use this practice while lying in bed. It has become normal for me to awaken with healing energy and to go to sleep with it. In my evening reflections, I generally focus on *forgiveness energy*, which helps to let go of any residual unwanted feelings or emotional energy. Using routines like these helps me to remain positively charged, so I can be a better conduit for the healing force.

When I conduct a session with a client, I make a direct energetic connection with that person by using my *BLESS method*, which I will describe in more detail in chapter four. This technique is an effective way to accurately read people's energy and help them accelerate their healing process. My specific healing ability has a lot to do with my dedication to help people improve their lives. While tapping into my natural gifts as a healer, I understand that the human mind is very powerful. Introducing the appropriate suggestions can have a tremendous influence on someone's mind-body energy. This is a fundamental principle in the creation of either disease or health.

When we feel inspired, it is as if our mind is being enlightened and prepared for a change. The word *inspiration* translates as *breathing in* and the breath of life exercise is therefore such an essential component of the healing process. The next chapter will give you more insight in how our mind operates and why hypnosis is such an effective tool to gain control over it.

Happy Memories from My Life

Thanks Mom & Dad for giving me Life, Love and Liberty

Chapter 2

IT's NOT WHAT YOU THINK

"Whatever you vividly imagine, ardently desire, sincerely believe in,
and enthusiastically act upon, must inevitably come to pass."

~ Ralph Waldo Emerson

Science of the Mind

Have you ever thought about how your mind works? Well, it's not *what* you think, it's more *how* you think and what you *feel* that matters. Support is rapidly growing for the paradigm that the mind is not just the brain but in fact part of every cell of our body. In her groundbreaking book *Molecules of Emotion*, neuroscientist and pharmacologist Candace Pert, Ph.D. says that *your brain is not in charge*. Dr. Pert's research focuses on decoding the *information molecules* such as peptides, and their receptors that regulate every aspect of human physiology. Dr. Pert has come to the conclusion that *your body is your subconscious mind.*

Another prominent scientist, stem cell biologist Bruce Lipton, Ph.D. and author of *The Biology of Belief,* explains that our DNA is controlled by signals from outside the cell, including the energetic messages from our positive and negative thoughts. Dr. Lipton's research shows that our bodies can be changed as we retrain our thinking. These important pieces of information support the premise of this book: *Using intuition, we can master our mind to promote healing energy.*

Healing occurs on many different levels: physical, mental, emotional, and spiritual. The decision and intention to heal is probably the most important step toward healing. The willingness to do whatever it takes to heal is the second most important. It allows you to make the necessary changes in your life. This willingness is directly linked to your ability to use your mind as a powerful tool to implement these changes. Making positive changes is much easier if you have some knowledge about the operating mechanism of your mind.

The Mind Model

Let's take a look at the human mind and use a simplified explanation of its operation system. We can understand our mind better by comparing it to a complex organic computer with three very distinct and separate functioning levels. Each has its own specific functions and storage capabilities. I will explain how your mind works using my interpretation of the mind model by one of my esteemed hypnosis teachers, Gerald F. (Jerry) Kein.

The human mind basically consists of three parts. The outer part is called the *conscious mind*, also known as our *thinking* mind. On the inner side we have the *subconscious mind*. We can call this our *feeling* mind. A deeper component of this part of the mind is called the *unconscious mind*. At this level, the automatic body functions such as our heartbeat and our immune system are controlled.

Creating positive change is not always easy because our mind programming is protected by what is known as the *Critical Faculty*. This aspect of the mind can be seen as a *Gatekeeper*, whose purpose it is to protect the existing program. It guards our *belief system* even if we consciously do not like that old belief or old truth anymore. The good news is that there are ways to bypass the Gatekeeper and start cultivating a new truth.

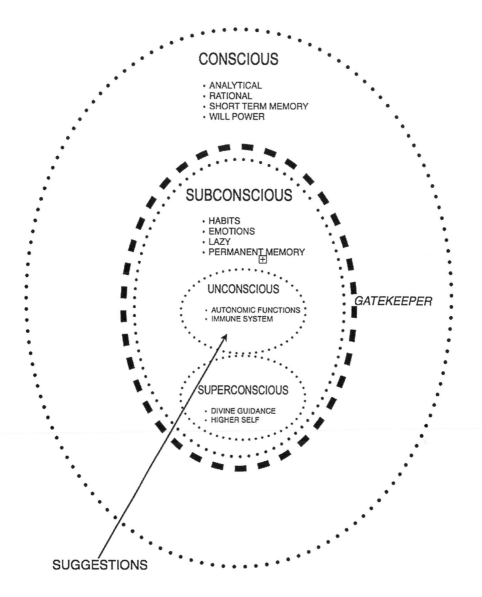

Conscious Mind

When we are awake, we focus much of our energy on our conscious mind. It has four different aspects

1. *Analyzing*

This means that the conscious mind looks at situations, puts the observed information together, and figures out a way to solve any challenges. It also helps us make hundreds of decisions to get through an average day. Decisions we may think are automatic in fact are not. These decisions include ones like, *Should I open this door? Should I turn the water on now? Should I go to work today?*

2. *Rationalizing*

This part of our conscious mind wants explanations for everything we do. It wants a reason why we behave in a particular way, even if it is a wrong reason such as *I smoke because it relaxes me.* Without a reason for our actions, we become tense, anxious and frustrated, and irrational. In the long run this could even lead to serious mental illness.

3. *Will Power*

We use our will consciously to achieve goals and finish projects. The problem in using will power is that it usually doesn't last very long. For example, we say that from now on we will exercise every day and we will, until our willpower weakens and the old habit pattern of inactivity returns. Also, by using willpower we put extra pressure on ourselves, which leads to increased stress levels and an overburdened nervous system.

4. *Memory*

Our *working* memory is the memory we need every day to answer questions such as, *What is my phone number? What is the name again of that person I just met? What did I have for dinner last night?* This conscious memory capacity is short-term, as opposed to the permanent memory found in the subconscious mind.

The conscious mind is the creator of all your attitudes and belief systems. It is responsible for reviewing and classifying everything you experience. It makes distinctions, it reasons, it limits you, it rationalizes, it edits, and it filters all of the information that it encounters. The conscious mind also judges, compares, and accepts or rejects information as being valid or not valid. It insures survival and prevents you from being overwhelmed with data by comparing it to your existing programs. It will reject data that does not fit with the programs that are already installed and operating.

Because the conscious mind creates and contains all of your judgements, it also governs all of your feelings and emotions. It assigns the emotional charge, positive or negative, to all of your life experiences. The conscious mind is the translator of all of your data as it is recalled from the subconscious mind. When it functions with accurate information, the conscious mind acts as your guardian and protector.

However, it can also be your greatest hindrance to healing and positive change, especially if during your early childhood it was fed negative, incorrect, or distorted data. Unfortunately, the conscious mind has the ability to deny obvious facts and might delete information vital to the healing process because of faulty beliefs. It is also able to resist or reject change, regardless of how positive the change will be on your life.

It is possible for your mind to accept new beliefs. If you can bypass the gatekeeper and access the data bank storage, you can reprogram and change your beliefs and associations. You can also compound any desired changes with positive affirmations, by unconditionally accepting the self, and acknowledging small positive changes as they are made. This helps your mind to realize that a positive result is being achieved.

To summarize what your conscious mind does: it is logical and analytical, and it stores your working memory and will power. The problem is that it is limited to sensory perception, thus frequently wrong and it often prevents you from making necessary changes.

Subconscious Mind

While the conscious mind can doze off, the subconscious mind never sleeps; it is always on. The subconscious mind is a super storage device that registers everything we go through in our life, even the things we are seemingly unaware of. Just like the conscious mind, it has four aspects.

1. *Habits*

We have three kinds of habits. Some are positive, some are negative, but most are utilitarian and they help us go through our day without having to think about every detail as if we are doing it for the first time. We automatically respond in a certain way. For example, when the telephone rings, we pick it up automatically without thinking.

2. *Emotions*

Depending on the programming your emotions may have more or less control over your life and can either help you or work against you. When emotions take over our rational thinking we lose our ability to reason and we may regret our actions later on.

3. *Laziness*

Although the subconscious mind is so powerful, it is also lazy and it doesn't like to facilitate change. It likes to keep things as they are and run the program. Changes to the program are not easily accepted. For example, the program says you are fat. If you stand in front of a mirror and think, *I am thin and attractive*, the subconscious mind rejects the suggestion initially because it does not match the program.

4. *Permanent Memory*

The subconscious mind has a super recorder that is always on. Everything that you have ever heard, seen, smelled, tasted, or felt is locked permanently into the memory banks of the subconscious mind. We never really forget anything. Using a specialized technique, called *regression* hypnosis, someone can travel back in time and review significant events that may have contributed to health problems in the present. This creates an opportunity for healing experiences.

The Gatekeeper

There is one more part of the mind that should not be overlooked. This part protects old programs from being replaced too easily. I mentioned it earlier and called it the *gatekeeper*. It is also known as the critical faculty, or critical factor. Its job is to protect any installed program from being deleted. The conscious mind communicates with the subconscious mind through our gatekeeper. Its job is to evaluate suggestions that want to enter the subconscious mind. The gatekeeper *must* protect us from danger, real or imagined, because the subconscious mind cannot distinguish between something actually happening or imagined to be happening.

In other words, to get new suggestions into our subconscious mind you or someone else first has to bypass your gatekeeper. There are a number of ways to do this. The most efficient way is to use hypnosis. It helps you to bypass the gatekeeper, so you can put new suggestions into your program. You are then able to review your old program, delete what no longer serves you, and replace the old program with a more suitable one. The process is very similar to uninstalling a computer program and installing a new one. Another option is to access the existing program and *download an upgrade.*

Authority figures such as doctors, preachers, teachers, and parents, as well as other people in powerful positions, must be aware of their ability to bypass the gatekeeping nature of the conscious mind. They can often tap directly into a person's subconscious mind. When this is done, whether for the person's benefit or not, most people will respond by going along with the authority's suggestion— usually without understanding why.

The power of the subconscious mind to accept suggestions from authority figures explains the impact of a physician's words on the healing process of a patient. A few key sentences spoken such as, *you are stronger than you imagine right now*, or *you are healing very quickly and doing extremely well,* can speed up the recovery process tremendously. On the negative side, statements such as *your cancer only has a 30 percent remission occurrence* can be accepted as a terminal prognosis and patients often die to the exact time limits their physicians gave them. Understanding the awesome power of the mind encourages us to use every positive means available to us to reprogram this amazing computer system.

Unconscious and Superconscious Mind

The subconscious and the *unconscious* parts of the mind are often incorrectly used as synonyms. The unconscious is actually a sublevel of the subconscious. After accessing the subconscious we can allow ourselves to move into a deeper level of trance, also known as *ultra-depth*, where we can influence our autonomic functions as well as our immune system.

The level of awareness called the *superconscious mind* is the part of us that is connected directly to your *divine guidance*. Through the superconscious mind, or *ultra-height*, we engage our *higher self*, and universal information and knowledge become available to us. Prayers are best sent and received through the superconscious mind and our vision may manifest as reality through this part of our mind. Prayer, visualization, and meditation can help us access this wonderful, limitless power. Healers tend to access this part of the mind to become a better conduit for the healing force.

Self-Hypnosis

A commonly heard phrase among hypnosis practitioners is *all hypnosis is self-hypnosis*. It indicates that, even though a person is in a state of heightened suggestibility, he or she will not lose *control* over their mind. The hypnotist serves as a guide to help facilitate the process and offer effective suggestions to establish change. The person in hypnosis has, at all times, the ability to select the appropriate suggestions or reject any words or phrases that are not useful.

Despite the Greek origin of the word hypnosis—*hypnos* means sleep—we are not asleep at all. In fact, all our five senses may dramatically improve in hypnosis and most people have much more awareness than in the conscious state of mind. The important thing to understand about this is that the conscious mind takes on a different role in this situation. We can say that it plays the role of *guardian angel*.

Because the subconscious mind operates like a super computer, it has recorded data of every instant of your life. In its memory card, all the colors, tastes, smells, sounds, sensations, and visuals of every event we have ever experienced are recorded in detail. It is capable of giving you a total recall of any event when you access this part of your mind. Through self-hypnosis, this recording can be played back, reviewed, and relived. With the guidance of a skilled practitioner, reactions and emotions can be healed and permanently reprogrammed through understanding, acceptance, and forgiveness. Once the subconscious mind is accessed, changes can occur fairly quickly and easily. Such changes facilitate the healing process and enable the body to heal.

Hypnosis and Healing

Humans are creatures of habit. Habits are created over time. Because you have learned to live with certain patterns and programs, you may have problems in breaking these patterns. It is usually easier to stay in the old pattern than to move forward with the healing process. Whenever you break an old habit pattern or clear an energy block, you create an opportunity for change. But this change, combined with the responsibilities that come with it, may have a tendency to bring up the emotion of fear. It is this fear, and the responsibilities incurred in changing, that you must face if you are to heal completely.

In the words of Norman Vincent Peale, "The sort of image you hold of yourself is very important, for that image will become fact. The thought is the ancestor of the deed. If you precondition your mind with thoughts of success, the deeds of success naturally tend to follow."

Almost all issues, symptoms, and illnesses are the exposed surface of much deeper causes. Healing just the surface symptoms only has a minimal effect on healing. Complete healing cannot occur until the root causes of the challenge have been addressed and resolved. If you can get in touch with and heal these root causes of your problem, your body knows how to heal.

We were all born with a sophisticated healing system. Ultimately, all can be healed if you are willing to do whatever it takes to heal.

Sometimes, however, part of us wants to continue drawing attention or has already given up because the root causes of the problem are never addressed.

Some people are so afraid of change that they would rather be sick or even die. That is sad, because with the right support making changes can actually enrich your life and make it better. If someone chooses to stop destroying him or herself, the next step is to decide to change negative feelings and negative self-talk. When we make a conscious choice to heal the destructive process, we can halt its progression and even reverse it.

Many times I have been privileged to help people heal completely. Each time is very different but it is always an extraordinary journey and a wonderful experience. Once we face our challenges and make a clear decision to heal, we tap into a source much greater than our own resources. The story below illustrates how the mind affected the healing process of a remarkable person who came to me for help and guidance.

Lillian's Story

My first question to Lillian was, "How do you feel I can help you best?" She looked at me hopefully and after a moment of silence she replied, "If only I could smile again." Three weeks before, she was diagnosed with ovarian cancer stage four. After emergency surgery, the oncologist had told her she would have only three months or less to live if she did not immediately start chemotherapy and even then her survival chances were grim. She was scared and felt more and more depressed as days full of confusion and nights without sleep went by. When Lillian came to me for healing work she was not expecting a cure for cancer; all she asked for was to regain some joy in her life. I felt confident about helping her feel better and I knew I could make her smile in our very first session.

During our pre-talk, I mentioned that I was born and raised in The Netherlands and Lillian's face lit up. She instantly remembered the wonderful vacation she had spent in my country of origin five years earlier and how she had loved walking through the flower fields of the famous Keukenhof. Our national symbol, the tulip, had become her favorite flower. I showed her a book with pictures of Dutch tulip fields and told her to hold on strongly to that image. For a moment she went back in time and a faint smile appeared on her face. Then I suggested that she close her eyes and imagine descending a staircase that would lead her right to that beautiful place. The smile became bigger and bigger as I guided her imagination through the park where she felt the joy again that she thought she had lost. When she returned from her first hypnotic experience she was still smiling and all she could say was, "Wonderful!"

As a fifty-four-year-old teacher of biology and chemistry, Lillian had always been fascinated by human physiology and psychology. The concept of mind-over-matter was not strange to her, but she had never considered herself a good subject for hypnosis. She thought of her mind as too analytical to allow another person to put her into trance. Lillian then discovered that her mind was very willing to accept my suggestions and, instead of vulnerable, she felt comfortable and in control. She decided to come for more sessions and also work closely together with my friend and associate, Dr. Sonja, for nutritional support and health education.

First, we worked on relaxation and helping Lillian sleep at night. After this, we started using hypnotic techniques that enabled her to influence her immune system, so her body could fight the *intruders*. When she chose to go through heavy chemotherapy, the combination of hypnosis and nutrition helped to keep her steady during the treatments. It also significantly reduced side effects such as nausea, vomiting, and hair loss. When the first round of chemo was completed, we were successful in boosting her white blood count using hypnotic imagery.

Reinforced by the mind work, Lillian amazed everyone with her positive attitude. She loved people and she actively continued her social life. I offered her the possibility of *regression to cause*, a way to explore the source of her illness by means of advanced hypnosis. The sessions we did revealed Lillian's deep-seated negative emotions toward her mother. They had been building up inside since before she was even born. In hypnosis, her mind took her back to a time she was still a fetus in the womb and she felt her mother's fear of having this baby.

Another *sensitizing event* that she reviewed occurred right after her birth: Her mother apologized to her father for not producing a son! Obviously, the woman was not aware that it's always the father's chromosome that determines a child's gender. Subsequently, Lillian's childhood was full of suppressed traumatic memories of her mother not accepting her child to be a girl. Her mother repeatedly called her ugly and fat. She had to wear boy's clothes and was scolded for sitting down on the toilet seat while urinating. Every day her mother obsessively washed the young girl's genital area, calling it "dirty". Later on, as a teenager, Lillian was warned almost daily about men, compounding the message that "all they want is sex." In her adult life she attracted men who reinforced this belief. Her second husband seemed to be different, but by now, she had denied herself feelings of intimacy and sex was non-existent in her marriage. Cancer is often regarded as "the body eating away on itself" and it was not surprising that the tumors appeared in the reproductive area of her body.

Lillian thought she had forgiven her deceased mother but she discovered that this was only true mentally, not emotionally. The conscious, thinking part of her mind knew that she had to move on, but in the subconscious, feelings of fear, sadness, anger, and resentment remained. A series of hypnosis sessions helped Lillian to release her hurt from the past. She was able to forgive many other people besides her mother, who all had given her feelings of being unwanted. Most importantly, she was able to forgive herself for denying her own womanhood. After disconnecting the emotional ties, Lillian's physical condition began to improve, surprising the various medical doctors who were monitoring her progress.

By now, Lillian had explored many healing modalities but she was most enthusiastic about hypnosis. As we continued our healing work to clean up residue of "old emotional stuff", Lillian decided she wanted to become a hypnotist and asked me to be her teacher. I felt honored to have such an inspiring student and our sessions became more and more spiritually oriented. It taught me a great deal about the many facets of hypnosis and it made me realize even more that we are all instruments of a higher power. Once we connect with that force, I believe we can move beyond our physical and emotional limitations.

Lillian became a certified hypnotist a year later, twenty months after the original medical prognosis of her death. She made her dream come true and was doing sessions to help people heal and improve the quality of their lives. Emotionally and spiritually she had transformed herself and her relationships with others. The medical test results showed no sign of cancer in her body and she lived every day with an attitude of gratitude. Lillian truly was an exceptional cancer patient who had experienced a miraculous healing.

Open Mind

I feel fortunate that people such as Lillian choose me as their healer. A person with an open mind is a delight to work with. A client's increased belief about one's positive outlook enables me to create a more effective healing environment. I am a healer but also a human being and just like other people I work better in a space where the flow of the healing force is unobstructed. That space can be the actual room we hold our session in or the imaginary space in someone's mind.

When people allow me access to their mind and give them suggestions for healing, we have already worked on increasing the level of trust that opens the doorway to the subconscious. Hypnosis is a wonderful power tool for healing and self-improvement when used appropriately and with the correct intent. If there is not a good energy connection between hypnotist and client, the mind cannot open enough and permanent positive change is very difficult to establish.

I am grateful for my natural ability to read a person's energy and to function as an effective healing conduit. However, the skills I have built on through my training are even more valuable. They have given me the tools to create rapport and move myself beyond perceived limitations. Healers can have off days just like everybody else. Fortunately, through proper experience and skills we are more equipped to either rebalance ourselves or temporarily suspend our own challenge to be an open, healing channel for others.

Keeping an open mind toward the extent of our own power is of vital importance. First and foremost, we all need to take care of ourselves in the same way we do for the people we help. It is not possible to function as a healer if you are running on empty. Second, it is essential to shield yourself from possible *energy leaks* or *energy thieves*. These can come in various forms, which I will describe in more detail in the next chapter.

Chapter 3

THE SUBTLE ENERGY SYSTEM

*"The physical world is a reflection of energy vibrations from more
subtle worlds that, in turn, are reflections of still more subtle energy fields.
Creation, and all subsequent existence, is a progression downward
and outward from the primordial source."*

~ Ervin Laszlo

The Nature of Energy

The word *energy* is derived from the ancient Greek word *energeia*, meaning *activity* or *operation*. Physical science has defined several forms of *kinetic* (motion) energy and *potential* (stored in matter) energy. These include thermal energy, chemical energy, electrical energy, radiation energy, nuclear energy, magnetic energy, elastic energy, sound energy, mechanical energy, and luminous energy.

What all these types of energy have in common is that their total energy contained in an object is identified with its mass, and energy (like mass) cannot be created or destroyed. When matter is changed into energy, the mass of the system does not change through the transformation process. Albert Einstein came to the following conclusion: One form of energy can be transformed into another. So, if one kind of energy has this characteristic, *all* forms of energy do.

During my training in various energy-healing modalities, my concept of energy shifted to the metaphysical aspect, in which *subtle energy* became the focus of my attention. For many years, the term *energy* has been widely used by writers and practitioners of esoteric forms of spirituality and complementary medicine. Subtle energy is often seen as a continuum that unites body and mind. It is conceived of as a universal life force running within and between all things.

This energy is spiritual in nature and often closely associated with the metaphor of the breath of life. The words *chi, qi, prana,* and *spirit* are all related to the verb *to breathe.* Often it is perceived with the movement of breath in the body, sometimes described as visible auras, *rays* or *fields,* or as audible or tactile vibrations.

In many cultural and religious traditions, the existence of esoteric energies is regarded as an *essence* that differentiates living from non-living objects. Subtle energy has become closely associated with concepts of animating spirits, or of the human soul. Some spiritual practices, such as qi gong or traditional yoga open or increase this innate energy and different forms of martial arts such as tai chi help to develop and focus subtle energy.

In my twenty-five years of experience as a healer I have come to the conclusion that a combination of conscious awareness, positive intent, and focused attention will always draw vital energy to the body that can produce extraordinary physical, psychological, and spiritual benefits.

To better define how a person's subtle energy behaves, I find it very useful to apply my intuitive perception to a framework such as the *auric field,* or the *chakra system.*

The Aura

The aura is a field of radiance that surrounds us like a halo. The complete aura consists of seven layers, known as *bodies,* identified as follows:

1. Physical Body

2. Emotional Body

3. Astral Body

4. Lower Mental Body

5. Higher Mental Body

6. Spiritual Body

7. Etheric Body

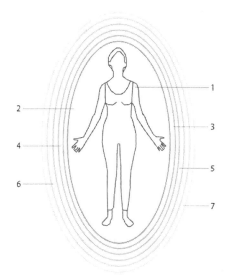

Those with well-developed intuitive abilities are able to detect luminous energy around a person. To a clairvoyant or master intuitive, the aura bodies may appear as various colors that each conveys a different meaning. Personally, I don't see auras very clearly but I do *feel* them quite strongly. I am clairsentient/clairaudient, meaning my intuitive sense of touch and hearing are more developed than my sight and I therefore don't rely too much on the color scheme that appears in my mind's eye when I read someone's energy.

I have discovered that auras are like mood rings that change with the emotional state we are in. It can change throughout the day from one moment to the next and is more or less a barometer for our emotional climate. Auras can be influenced by events or the energies of other people. The bodies tend to shrink when we feel intimidated and expand when we are empowered. When two people are in love they feel their auras merge and amplify, which will cause observers to make remarks like, "she looks radiant!" or "he was beaming!"

Celebrities, politicians, and leaders in general tend to have an aura that is wide and thick, especially when they are performing or addressing a group. We sometimes call this strong expansion of the auras *charisma*.

However, the same people may, in another setting, become frightened and powerless, causing their aura bodies to shrink and become thinner. Unhealthy people tend to show dark-colored areas in their aura and those with healthy body-minds can emanate light hues of violet, white, and gold.

Below is an aura picture of me taken with special photographic equipment in 1995. I was having a great time teaching a class in energy healing and in the lunch break, we all had our aura photo taken at a psychic fair nearby. The Native American man who took the photo and gave an intuitive interpretation was very enthusiastic that practically all colors of the spectrum showed up— usually one or two colors are dominant.

My colors indicated the ability to transform others through compassion, dedication, peace, trust, honesty, and love. What he had never seen before though was the so-called *Celtic Cross* intersecting at the top of my head, indicating a strong healing potential. He asked me if I had any inclination to work in the healing field and he was pleased to hear that I had already been on that path for over 10 years.

For a moment I wondered if there might have been a technical glitch. However, none of the other people in the group had an aura picture that resembled the colors in my photo. There were no horizontal or vertical beams in any of the others pictures that were taken either before or after mine.

When I enthusiastically told my mentor, Dr. Sonja, what had happened and proudly showed her my picture, she looked at me with a curious smile. Then, she pulled out a binder from a drawer and opened it on a page where she kept an aura photo of herself taken years earlier. My jaw literally dropped when I saw the same Celtic Cross showing up in her picture! "I imagine you and I may have to join our healing forces," she said.

Dr. Sonja explained to me that the subtle energy of the aura can be positively manipulated through color energy enhancement, energy work, meditation, or changing one's surroundings. When these images were taken, we were each in an enhanced healing state with an optimized energetic flow.

Many of the methods in this book can positively influence the way your aura behaves, especially the one I will describe in chapter seven. Always be aware that the aura radiates from your body and is an expression of your current state of being. For more profound and permanent changes you need to work on your *chakras*.

The Chakras

Chakras are energy centers in the subtle human energy system that can either have a low, neutral, or high vibrational quality. They are influenced by inner as well as outer events. The word chakra is Sanskrit for *wheel* or *disc*, meant to move and not become stagnated or stuck. The original concept originated in Hindu texts, featured in tantric and yogic traditions of Hinduism and Buddhism. While auras can be adjusted based on mood and intent, your chakras are more anchored and rooted. They reflect your current areas of strength and weakness and tell the story of your life.

There are hundreds, perhaps thousands of chakras in and outside the human body, but generally we simplify the framework into seven major chakras:

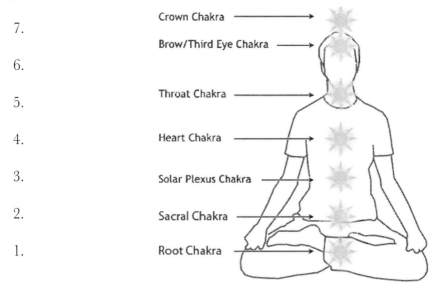

7.   Crown Chakra ⟶

6.   Brow/Third Eye Chakra ⟶

5.   Throat Chakra ⟶

4.   Heart Chakra ⟶

3.   Solar Plexus Chakra ⟶

2.   Sacral Chakra ⟶

1.   Root Chakra ⟶

Chakras are regarded as *powerhouses* in the way they generate and store energy, with universal energy pulled in more strongly at these points. Each chakra in our spinal column influences and governs bodily functions near its region of the spine. They begin at the base of the spinal column and move upward to the top of the skull. Chakras are considered to be intersections of human bio-energy. This life force energy is the basic component of your subtle body, your energy field and the entire chakra system, the key to life, and source of energy in the universe.

Chakra Balancing

Scanning and balancing chakras has been an essential part of my practice for many years. The way I perceive a chakra is more as a *sphere,* multi-dimensional, and able to transmit and receive energy in many different forms. When I conduct a session with a client, the purpose is always to optimize that person's self-healing/self-improving capacity. A session can take anywhere from thirty minutes to two hours. After the initial interview, clients lie comfortably on a massage table, usually face-up as I guide them through relaxing imagery. Then I start *tuning in.* This intuitive process can be compared to finding the right channel on a radio receiver and then amplifying the signal.

My intuitive abilities combined with my skills in hypnosis, music, and energy healing help me to hear and feel signals sooner than I see them. Sometimes images and words are revealed to me and/or my client and sometimes I feel the energy as warmth or sensations that are flowing to and from different parts of the body. To amplify and optimize the healing effect, I may use guided imagery, hypnosis, Tibetan bowls or other instruments, therapeutic touch, crystals/gemstones, aromatherapy, or I produce toning sounds with my voice. The aim of a session is to create balance within the subtle energy system. As a result, my clients can go back into their world looking and feeling refreshed and recharged with a sense of calmness and peace.

Chakras and Emotions

Clients often come in with a clear medical diagnosis. Almost always I find there is also an imbalance of either an emotional or spiritual nature. When I scan for either *plus* or *minus* areas, a polarity of words begins to flow through my mind. I am especially interested in the emotional aspects of my clients' chakras because these feelings have an immediate effect on our wellbeing. If we identify them correctly we can efficiently influence them in a way we choose. As human beings, we don't always have the desire to feel calm and relaxed. There are times when we may want to feel excited and sometimes we may even wish we could become angry—for instance, if we want to stand up for ourselves. The keyword is *control*. Being in control of your emotions will empower you and help you evolve from who you *used* to be to whom you *choose* to be.

Here is an overview of each chakra and a success story of clients I have worked with and how their healing process evolved around that particular energy center.

Chakra 1

Original name: Maladhara
Western name: Root or Base chakra
Gland(s):   Reproductive/Gonads
System: Skeletal
Color: Red

The emotional connection of the Root Chakra may evolve around:

- Giving & Receiving
- Security & Support
- Stability & Groundedness
- Family, Group, Community
- Survival & Self-Preservation

Hank's Root Chakra Story

When I met Hank for the first time he came for an in-office session. He wanted to release the underlying reason for his procrastination. Throughout his life he had often postponed making important decisions that could give direction to his life. Feeling stuck, Hank was looking for motivation to change this pattern. He realized that his belief system needed an upgrade and he contacted me for assistance with that.

After our initial interview, I helped Hank move into a state of deep tranquility where his mind was more receptive to my suggestions. During the first part of the session, Hank went from a state of nervousness (twitching, couching, moving around, shallow breathing) to relaxation as he followed my suggestions. From there I took him deeper into his subtle energy system with sounds and touch.

When I scanned his energy I strongly sensed a tremendous depletion in his lower chakra region. Zooming in more, I found an energetic block in chakra one, almost like a *dam* keeping his life force from being renewed and at the same time holding on to old beliefs and old hurt. Using my skills, my healing tools, and my positive intent, I gently directed *recharged energy* to the area.

At the end of our session Hank told me about images of the past that had come up and revealed the source of his belief barriers. There were many situations in which he had felt blocked, locked up or confined. These sensitizing events related to family drama and group conflicts that had caused him to feel isolated, which prevented him from moving forward. He had also gotten images of the future where he would no longer have that restriction.

Hank joked that I was helping him do the reverse of the story where the Dutch boy held his finger in the dam. We laughed first and then decided that in his case, a breakthrough was necessary to release his personal obstructions. Following my structured individual program, Hank was now ready to build his life on the new foundation we established in his root chakra.

Chakra 2

Original name:	Swadhistana
Western name:	Sacral chakra
Gland:	Adrenals
Systems:	Reproductive & Excretory
Color:	Orange

The emotional connection of the sacral chakra may evolve around:

- Guilt & Shame
- Pleasure & Sexuality
- Personal Identity & Creativity
- Cycles of Change & New Beginnings
- Identifying & Releasing Toxic Relationships

Melanie's Sacral Chakra Story

When Melanie called for an appointment, I remembered her from ten years ago. Then, she was in her early twenties and had been suffering from severe PMS basically from the time she got her first period at age twelve. A combination of reflexology/energy work and a personalized nutritional program designed by Dr. Sonja had completely normalized her menstrual cycles in only a few months' time.

With renewed hopefulness for the future she had found a job out of state and a man to share her life with. Unfortunately, they did not live happily ever after. The husband turned out to be a person with many issues and addictions that, over the years, made him more and more abusive. Eventually, Melanie ended up in the hospital twice, after which she filed for divorce.

Melanie decided to move back to the east coast and after a few years she met Larry, who was the polar opposite of her ex-husband. She finally married this caring and supportive man and they decided to start a family. Even though the conditions now seemed optimal for Melanie to become pregnant, she started having all kinds of problems relating to her sacral chakra: frequent urinary tract irritation and infection, heavy menstrual cramps and bleeding, lower back discomfort, sciatica, and an inability to conceive. Emotionally, she was in a downward spiral that affected her every move. Larry encouraged her to use the same approach that she used in the past to reclaim her life. If it worked for her then, there was a big chance it would work again.

And so, Melanie called me for a session. I suggested we start with some reflexology since she had experienced such a good response with that approach in the past. I did a chakra scan using energy points on the feet and hers had quite a story to tell. I sensed a great sadness that had been with her for many years, affecting her ability to feel good about herself and fully enjoy her life. As I worked on one pressure point, corresponding with her uterus, she suddenly had a flash of insight that related to her childhood, age seven or eight. A memory that she had suppressed for many years came to her very vividly. An adult relative had molested her and told her it was her fault because she was teasing him as she was dancing to music.

I helped Melanie release the emotional connection as she started to become more and more aware of how this event had affected her life in many ways. Even though she enjoyed listening to music, she had always been extremely anxious when asked to dance and even developed sciatic pain on her prom night! I explained to her that moving our hips rhythmically to sound is an expression of celebration. It is natural and healthy for human beings to dance and it helps us be in touch with our creative energy center. Melanie began to realize how she had attracted abusive people in her life that reinforced her childhood secret. It even caused her to have extreme pain and discomfort in her sacral chakra region for many years.

She had already started to break through this pattern by marrying Larry. Now it was time for Melanie to disconnect from the source of this old hurt and forgive those who had hurt her, including herself. Feeling pleasure naturally became her new quest and we did some specific follow-up sessions to speed up the process. Her creativity received an enormous boost as well, and two months after Melanie and Larry took up ballroom dancing together she sent me a note saying, "My creativity is definitely flowing again, feeling alive and happy and . . . I just found out I am expecting a baby, the ultimate creation! Thank you for all your help."

Chakra 3

Original name:	Manipura
Western name:	Solar Plexus chakra
Gland:	Pancreas
Systems:	Digestive & Muscular
Color:	Yellow

The emotional connection of the solar plexus chakra may evolve around:

- Joy & Frustration
- Acceptance & Resentment
- Success & Job Dissatisfaction
- Enthusiasm & Discouragement
- Low Self-Esteem

Anthony's (Tony's) Solar Plexus Story

I met Tony around this time last year. December was not exactly his favorite month. At his initial session with me he said he dreaded the holidays like nothing else and he would rather spend a few weeks in the hospital than endure the "agony of Christmas and New Year and all that goes on around it."

"Really? How come?" I replied. Tony continued to explain that, even though he loved his wife dearly, he couldn't stand her family. Ever since he married Eileen fourteen years ago, her parents, brothers, and sisters had been making demeaning remarks about him, suggesting he was not good enough for her. In their opinion, Tony did not have the right background and education and he was not wealthy enough to give her the life she deserved. Their comments were so subtle and covert that he started to believe them and it took its toll on his marriage, his work, and his health.

Eileen had bought her husband a gift certificate for a session with me. "A gift of love," she had called it. To her it didn't matter what anyone else said. Anthony was her soulmate and their bond was forever. All she wanted was for her husband to feel joyful again. He had been quite successful as an independent insurance agent, steadily increasing his business and attracting clients with his reassuring enthusiasm and convincing voice.

Over the past few years though, Tony's self-confidence started to diminish and so did his business. He became frustrated about his work in the world. Worried about his income, he took on a second job, which caused extra stress and fatigue. As Tony was holding in all of his emotions, he started having problems in his body that reflected this, such as constipation and weight gain. He also felt very weak in his muscles, not the strong guy he used to be. Most of all, he felt like he had forgotten how to be the man he always liked to be.

"What can you do for me?" Tony asked me. I answered with the question, "Are you willing to do whatever it takes?" After ten seconds of silence, Tony said, "I'm ready." The determination in his voice told me he realized what was at stake: his sense of self, his health, his life.

First, we did a bio-energetic assessment for emotions. Tony was fascinated with what came up and found it to be right on. Second, a chakra scan and reading, during which I gave him hypnotic suggestions to build self-confidence and joy. Third, I strongly recommended him to go on an exercise program (eight minutes per day) and change his diet.

I suggested he make an appointment with Dr. Sonja. It was very important to start doing this before the temptations of the holidays. In the past few years Tony had gained extra pounds during this season because— like for many other people—(comfort) food seemed to be the only way for him to counterbalance the stress, anxiety, and feelings of low self-worth.

By mid-December we had done four sessions and Tony had found his internal smile again. He had lost five pounds and his strength was back. He was actually looking forward to celebrating the holidays. His business was picking up, but he felt like going in a new direction. Tony continued working with me on his solar plexus by doing my personal development program. I coached him into finding his core values, his soul's intention and his life purpose.

Nowadays he introduces himself with his full name Anthony, representing his new self— also the name Eileen always preferred. "It just feels better," he says. Anthony is considering a career change. He took my HypnoCourse and became a certified hypnotist. With his reassuring radiance and his comforting confidence, he'll do great!

Chakra 4

Original name:	Anahata
Western name:	Heart chakra
Gland:	Thymus
Systems:	Cardiovascular & Lymphatic
Color:	Green

The emotional connection of the Heart chakra may evolve around:

- Love & Passion
- Balance & Vitality
- Defense & Protection
- Compassion & Nurturing
- Self- & Global Awareness

Aurora's Heart Chakra Story

It was mid October 1999 and every day of the month Aurora had faithfully worn a pink ribbon to give attention to Breast Cancer Awareness Month. A neighbor and a distant cousin of hers had both been diagnosed with the disease and she had been supporting them through their challenge in any way she could. This morning, Aurora had an uneasy feeling when she held the adornment in her hand. After her husband Matthew had left for the office and her two young children were off to school, she decided to do a self-examination, which confirmed her premonition. She felt something in her left breast that wasn't there before, something that didn't feel good at all.

Aurora felt like calling her husband, but she realized that Matthew had an important meeting that morning and she didn't want to disturb him. Who else could help her ease this distress? Her mother was ailing and too weak to offer advice, and other relatives generally relied on her to be their counselor. Close friends she really didn't have, because her responsibilities as a "domestic goddess" consumed most of her days and nights. A combination of sadness, anxiety, and loneliness welled up but she quickly suppressed the emotions by telling herself that it's *probably nothing serious and it will go away by itself*. She was wrong. That night she told Matthew and, at his insistence, she decided to see a doctor. Later that week medical tests confirmed that the lump in her breast was malignant and had to be removed ASAP.

After the surgery, an emotional rollercoaster followed and Aurora felt very confused, unsteady, uncertain about what to do next. Treatment protocols were suggested, including medication and radiation. It all seemed so unreal to her, as if it was happening to someone else. She needed more time to reflect before making any decisions. Suddenly, it dawned upon her that she had become an expert at being there for others but she had not built up a support system for herself. So far, Aurora had always been able to handle personal setbacks by herself, now it was time to ask others to help her. The more she asked, the more she received and it became clear to her that it was important to work on her inner self, not just her body. She considered learning to meditate, and her cousin referred her to me.

When Aurora came in for her first session, I asked her how she felt I could help her best. She answered, "I want to feel safe inside myself again." I explained that for this to happen, she had to connect with the part of her that had contributed to the formation of this lump. I helped her jumpstart the process through a series of hypnosis and chakra-balancing sessions.

First I used general suggestions for healing, but in our follow-up appointments the imagery was targeted at finding the underlying cause. By now it became clear that the core of the imbalance was located in her heart chakra. Not only are the breasts located in this energy center, it also deals with imbalances in the lymphatic system and immune system. Furthermore, the heart chakra helps to circulate our vitality through the cardiovascular system. All of this was affected, because with cancer, the body turns against itself.

I suggested we do a hypnotic review session. In a deep state of hypnosis, Aurora went back to age nine when her alcoholic father had just died in a car accident. That morning, she had yelled at her dad and smashed a bottle of vodka, after which he told her she was "a hateful child without love in her heart." The only way to deal with her mixed emotions of anger, heartbreak, and guilt was to suppress them and take care of her mother and sister who were even more distraught. As she grew up, Aurora continued taking care of others in an overly compassionate and supportive way, while at the same time denying her own need to feel loved.

After nine years of marriage Matthew had begun to find his daily bottle of wine more appealing than his wife and the love part had faded out of their relationship. In her marriage Aurora relived the relationship with her father only to go through the same pain again. Through this chakra healing session Aurora was ready to face the memories of her past and begin a process of forgiveness. She was now ready release the fixation to nurture others and embrace her life with love and compassion for herself and share her true self with others.

Over the years, Aurora's life has changed in many ways. She has changed her diet, her lifestyle, and her mindset. She has been using Dr. Sonja's nutritional guidance for many years and without the use of medical procedures, other than her initial lumpectomy, she has been cancer-free for six years now. The love is back in her partnership with Matthew. He stopped drinking and is working from home where he shares in the domestic responsibilities, including raising the kids. This enabled Aurora to go back to school and become a licensed massage therapist, using her natural ability to nurture in a professional way. She finds it tremendously therapeutic for herself.

Chakra 5

Original name:	Vishuddha
Western name:	Throat chakra
Gland:	Thyroid
System:	Respiratory
Color:	Blue

The emotional connection of the Throat chakra may evolve around:

- Truth & Dishonesty
- Appreciation & Criticism
- Personal Expression & Shyness
- Assertiveness & Lack of Will Power
- Listening & Communication Problems

Jackie's Throat Chakra Story

I first met Jackie when she was only ten-years-old. She had been chosen for a leading part in a school musical, which made her very nervous.

Even though she had a wonderful, natural singing voice, under pressure she felt very anxious, which constricted her throat and she started losing her voice from pushing too hard. She developed white spots on her vocal chords called nodules, which added to the problem. "Jackie," I said, "I know just what to do about that."

Then I told her my own story of being an eleven-year-old boy who had that same problem. My mom took me to a speech pathologist that taught me wonderful techniques. It was called self-hypnosis, and I practiced and practiced every day until the white spots started disappearing.

In a few sessions I instructed Jackie to do the same thing I had done and soon the nodules were all gone and her voice came back stronger than ever. She also found out that the techniques worked for all kinds of other things like sleep problems, nervousness, trouble concentrating, nausea, stomach pains, and headaches.

When Jackie called me a few months ago, she said, "I believe I need a tune-up." She told me that she was taking her passion for music to a professional level. She was a talented twenty-year-old background singer in a rock band. She confided in me that her biggest fear had always been to disappoint her father, who had failed with a career in music himself. He was always pushing her to become a better singer, but kept criticizing her performance with mean and abusive language. Interestingly, she was in a relationship with one of the members of the band who treated her the same way.

Jackie was on prescription anti-anxiety medication and anti-depressants and she sometimes took sleeping pills. I suggested we do a thorough chakra balancing session to get her body and mind back into harmony and find a new healthy rhythm for her life to move into. In that session her throat chakra revealed a tremendous energetic blockage that prevented her from expressing her heart song and only bringing out the resentment and frustration in a raw and angry way. In our session, we did a toning segment that helped release past hurt and bring out the purity of her voice.

After this session, Jackie began to understand that it was up to her to change her life, follow her own will and desires, and make her own choices and decisions. She now chooses to determine the direction of her life and is doing my mind mapping program (see chapter six) to help her to better use her talents and abilities and let go of self-imposed limitations. Jackie has left the rock band and is now the lead singer in her own band. The relationship with her father is improving— a work in progress. She is off all medication and into meditation as well as a healthy lifestyle. Her new boyfriend adores her voice and everything else about her.

Chakra 6

Original name: Ajna
Western name: Brow or Third Eye chakra
Gland: Pituitary
System: Endocrine
Color: Indigo

The emotional connection of the Brow chakra may evolve around:

- Dreams & Fears
- Focus & Distraction
- Knowledge & Ignorance
- Vision & Loss of Direction
- Peace of Mind & Overwhelm

Julia's Brow Chakra Story

When Julia came to me for energy healing she was in a depressed state of mind. Over the previous few months she had been spiraling down into negativity, and every new day she felt worse than the day before. She had seen an endocrinologist for many years who had prescribed medication for her low-functioning thyroid. Six months ago, at age forty-two, she was also diagnosed with type-two diabetes. Julia understood that being overweight was an important contributing factor and she vowed to change her eating habits and start exercising regularly.

That intent was good but after five days, she fell back into her old program and her eating habits became even worse. Instead of reducing weight she gained more and more pounds and eventually became morbidly obese. "I am not even hungry," she said, "but I keep wanting to eat more. What's wrong with me?" I explained to her that she was being robbed by thieves, *energy thieves*, and that it would not surprise me if there were subconscious energy manipulators at work as well. The good news was that the intruders could be eliminated using the latest technology and energy healing.

Through a personal energy evaluation I was able to determine the exact values of Julia's energy field and which energy center, or chakra, was mostly affected. It showed that she had a strong emotional conflict in her sixth chakra that was stealing her personal energy on all levels. This area, also known as the brow chakra or third eye, governs the endocrine system through its main gland, the pituitary, often called the *master gland*.

The conflict was a result of a lifetime of negative relationships that started in her childhood with both parents using sarcasm, belittlement, and criticism to exert authority over their children. Julia was unable to metabolize these experiences, which contributed to her thyroid condition. But the deeper underlying message of not deserving happiness developed as a systemic endocrine disease. Without dissolving this deep emotional conflict it was impossible for Julia to develop enough self-discipline to form new, healthy habits.

As part of her session, a clearing took place that opened up a new healing pathway for Julia. We followed up using review hypnosis to reframe the subconscious manipulations that were installed by others. It enabled her to speak her own truth, develop willpower and self-control, and heal her past.

Over the next three months, Julia's thyroid and diabetes conditions stabilized. She went down six sizes and found new sweetness in dating a really nice guy called Jeremy. He treats her with respect and has a great sense of humor, which also helps her to love and accept herself completely.

Chakra 7

Original name:	Sahasrara
Western name:	Crown chakra
Gland:	Pineal
System:	Neurological
Color:	Violet

The emotional connection of the Crown chakra may evolve around:

- Faith & Distrust
- Hope & Despair
- Wisdom & Impulsivity
- Spirituality & Fanaticism
- Surrendering & Defiance

Doug's Crown Chakra Story

Doug was the oldest son of a successful businessman. Both his parents came from a modest background but they worked their way up in life and now they belonged to an affluent community. As a result, they wanted nothing but the best. As he grew older, Doug was prepared by them to be a worthy representative.

He told me during his initial visit, "All my life I have felt this pressure to be a super achiever. I am thirty-two-years-old and I can't slow down." Doug was on anti-anxiety medication and said that he had always felt rushed. There was never time to stop and smell the roses, or to simply feel his feelings. He needed to be fully competent and successful in the illusionary world his parents had created and it literally gave him migraine headaches.

His brain was burning with unrealistic expectations that he took over from his parents. Doug realized he was even projecting it onto his own children. He was on medications for anxiety, sleeplessness, and erectile dysfunction, but he wanted to find a different, more natural way to improve his health and get to know his true self. I suggested a personal energy evaluation program. I explained to him that chronic conditions can be caused by energy blocks. They usually result from suppressed emotional conflicts. These conflicts block the flow of energy in the body, which leads to health complaints and illness.

It is often not enough to bring these issues into the conscious mind. They need to be resolved in the body's subtle energy field where it is stored as a pattern. Here it leads an energetic life of its own, depleting your energy reserves and contributing to physical and/or mental imbalances.

In Doug's case this approach, helped to discover a strong imbalance in his crown chakra. This energy center governs the nervous system, which had been challenged all his life and eventually started to manifest physical symptoms. Without this awareness, Doug's nervous system grid might have collapsed and become frozen. This may contribute to diseases such as MS, Parkinson's or Alzheimer's.

After his session Doug felt like a new person. The crown chakra can be strengthened through a connection with a higher source of power and he learned to tune in to different messages than the ones he got while growing up. He listened to a song that Dr. Sonja and I wrote, called *Faith, Hope and Love*, which really resonated with him.

Over the next few months, Doug gradually developed his authentic self and, nowadays, even meditates daily. He goes for long, contemplative walks in nature and he is exploring his spiritual side. He says, "I was going too fast and I only knew life superficially. I feel that finally I am starting to live and I love being real!"

Personal Energy Evaluation

Julia's and Doug's chakra stories refer to the latest development in subtle energy healing, an innovative technology from Switzerland. It is called the *personal energy evaluation*, an advanced method to help people go to the next level of fine-tuning, clearing, and balancing their energy centers. I find this modern approach exciting and complementary to my own skills and intuitive abilities. It helps me to specifically assess the value of energy blocks and emotional energy conflicts that can cause both acute and chronic disease. The different energy levels that are tested are:

Vital

This corresponds to the amount of strength a person physically has at his disposal. A person with a low vital energy level is generally exhausted much of the time.

Emotional

This corresponds to a person's mood. Someone with a low emotional energy generally feels grumpy, irritated, overly sad, or emotionally depleted.

Mental

This corresponds to a person's conscious awareness. It is what allows him to get through the day efficiently. Someone with a low mental level generally is forgetful, easily distracted, and has trouble concentrating.

Causal

This corresponds to the person's intuition and inner guidance. The higher the causal level, the more sensitive, intuitive, and connected he is with the world around him. Identified emotional conflicts can be cleared energetically. The aim is to gradually and completely rebalance a person's subtle energy system. This process may take a number of months as we are going to different levels of healing, just like peeling away layers of an onion.

The results I have seen using this method are amazing, especially when followed up with modalities such as reflexology, polarity therapy, reiki, light touch massage, and hypnosis. I obtained advanced certifications in these and various other forms of therapeutic massage and energy work.

In my experience, what makes any of these approaches effective is the level of intuitive perception a practitioner can bundle to use the most effective technique(s).

Subtle Energy Facilitators

Finding a practitioner who is skilled in all of the above modalities and who can facilitate your healing process is not always easy. And even when you have found someone with all the credentials you are looking for, you still may not feel energetically connected to that person. It's important to work with a healer who can help create the best environment to optimize your healing process.

Some of my clients see me only for a few sessions. With others I may embark on a spiritual journey that involves both healing and self-actualization. By engaging our *intuitive perception* we get together to create a *new normal* using any tools and skills at our disposal to reach for and maintain this new level of consciousness and wellbeing.

Traditionally, those people who work with me are referred via word of mouth, but more and more clients find their way to me by engaging their own *intuition*. Perhaps nowadays they are using an Internet search engine to start with, but the decision-making process on where to go for help is usually very intuitive. If the energy feels right, that person probably *is* right for you at that moment.

Chapter 4

INTUITIVE PERCEPTION

"There is no logical way to the discovery of these elemental laws.
There is only the way of intuition, which is helped by a feeling
for the order lying behind the appearance."

~ Albert Einstein

Intuition

I use the term *intuition* to describe a knowing, a sensing without conscious thought. It is perception of knowledge via the unconscious with no analytical reasoning. The word intuition comes from the Latin word *intuere*, which is often translated as *to look inside* or *to contemplate*. Intuition provides us with information that comes from a *gut feeling*. According to Rudolph Steiner, intuition is the third of three stages of higher knowledge, after imagination and inspiration. Typically, intuition is regarded as a conscious commonality between earthly knowledge and the higher spiritual knowledge, appearing as flashes of insight or illumination.

In other words, it's not what you think. Logical reasoning it's not, but it certainly is an essential aspect of my work as a healer. Without engaging my intuitive perception, I would get a completely different reading and not the same result in a session. The insights I get through my intuitive perception usually build up during a reading and form and shape into images and words until enough pieces of the puzzle fall into place. While conducting energy work or doing hypnosis, I then bring an appropriate message to my client. Often I have an *epiphany*, a sudden moment of clarity when an important part of the energy that comes through appears to me as a revelation. Very often this experience goes along with an energizing jolt, a vibrational frequency that moves me into a light trance. I have learned to accept this feeling as *a good thing*, because it confirms the optimal energetic state to work from as an instrument for the healing force.

As a session progresses, I intend to establish an exchange of energy with my client. This means that the healing energy that flows through me can find its way through our aura connection into the chakra system of the other person. At the same time, that person may have *unwanted* (not necessarily negative) energy to release. When this happens, I usually experience temporary tiredness, tearing eyes, shifts in body temperature, and tightness in certain body parts. Burping and flatulence can also be added to the list, but I have learned to keep these under control for obvious reasons. It helps to know how to apply self-hypnosis.

Rather than telling you, "Do not try this at home," I would like to encourage you to become more familiar with your own intuitive potential. I believe the world could be a better place if everyone could move into a more mindful intuitive state at will. I envision our collective consciousness rising and humanity shifting to a level of what Eckhart Tolle describes as *awakened doing* in his book *A New Earth*. He defines it as three modalities: *acceptance* of the past, *enjoyment* of the present, and *enthusiasm* for the future.

I resonate with his teachings and perhaps my method can contribute to this positive development when more people apply it. I explain it in detail below but before you try it, there is another important guideline to follow when engaging your intuition for the purpose of healing, self-improvement, or maybe only for your entertainment. It is called *shielding*, an important skill to develop to help protect your personal energy from negativity and external attack.

Negative People

Have you ever wondered why being around certain people makes you feel tired or even sick, although they don't appear to have a negative intent toward you? Chances are you are dealing with what is called a *negative person*. Negative people may display any of the following traits:

- Complain about life in general
- Have a self-victimizing mindset
- Look for problems rather than solutions
- Leave other people around them drained
- Counter any remark with a negative opinion
- Are focused on what is wrong and who is to blame

These people can be regarded as *energy vampires* because they are not capable of generating their own positive life force and therefore feed off other people's energy. Also, they have a strong urge to change you and others into one of them— someone who is miserable, lonely, and stuck. The reason for this is that they have become blocked off from the universal life force and often feel victimized because their inner source of power is depleted.

A negative person should not be mistaken for a *critical person*. Critical people highlight things they don't like or approve of. An energy vampire doesn't like life in general.

Aura Shielding

Shielding your aura is an effective way to form an energy protection layer and protect your aura from energy vampires. An *aura shield* is a force field or a bubble around you that keeps your energy to yourself and prevents it from any intruders or undesirable energy to enter your space. Just like a real shield, a subtle energy shield is a defense tool that may wear off over time so you need to replace it regularly. I create my most effective aura shields as follows:

The Seven-Step Shielding Method

1. Close your eyes and take three deep breaths
2. Rub your hands together until they feel warm and/or tingly
3. Create the image of an energy ball between your hands
4. Let the energy ball expand and surround you
5. Check the shield for any weak spots and strengthen them
6. Fill the shield with protective white light
7. Enjoy meeting people, and feeling safe and confident

Compassion

With your shield up you will still be able to receive positive energy. Consider the force field you created for your aura semi-permeable. A force field that is too strong may close you off too much which could inhibit your positive connection to the world around you.

Once your shield is firmly in place you may be able to extend a helping hand to a negative person. Initially, you may not receive much appreciation but if you keep the topic of conversation light and use humor you may notice gradual shifts in that person's behavior. Using the energy of *compassion* helps you to keep your energy from being robbed. Compassion is when you wish that the other person would not have to suffer, but you are able to distance yourself from their issue. Even though you grace the other person with your presence, you remain the observer. It is more draining to use *empathy* and take on part of the suffering of the victim.

The BLESS Method

Now you are well prepared to use your intuition for the purpose of *energy reading* or *scanning*. My BLESS method is a powerful technique that will enable you to make an accurate intuitive impression of your own, or another person's energy flow, using the chakra system as your guide and universal life force energy as your amplification device.

```
┌─────────────────────────────┐
│                             │
│           BLESS             │
│                             │
│         BREATHE             │
│          LINK               │
│        ENERGIZE             │
│          SINK               │
│          SCAN               │
│                             │
└─────────────────────────────┘
```

BREATHE

Breathing is not just a way to get oxygen into the body. Through our breath we create a flow of air that is both refreshing and releasing. By creating breath awareness we become more mindful and present, and begin to shift our focus from *nowhere* to *now here*.

Imagine your lungs filling up with inspiration as you breathe in and then let go of whatever does not serve you as you breathe out. It's important to take at least three long, deep breaths and either do this with the eyes closed or while gazing at an area in front of you.

LINK

To be able to become an open channel for universal healing energy we need to form a link with a higher power. This could be God, Nature, The Universe, All That Is, Spirit, The Source, or any other concept your mind can accept and believe in.

Imagine an antenna, satellite dish, or other receptor at your crown chakra that you direct upward. When the connection is made it is common to feel a shudder or other mild sensation going through your body as your nervous system establishes the link, similar to a computer connecting to Wi-Fi.

ENERGIZE

Now that you have established your link, allow the source to energize your soul so the positive energy you need to help others can come *through* you instead of *from* you.

Imagine this energy coming in through the top of your head, or the crown chakra, in the form of bright light and feel how it fills your entire body up with grace, as if you are tapping into a reservoir of goodness. This experience is comparable to going into trance.

SINK

Just as we create trance depth during a hypnotic induction, it is important to allow for a deepening of the healing energy, so it can find its way to your core, where your true values are located.

Imagine descending a staircase or escalator, or taking an elevator down to a place that symbolizes your heart space, a sanctuary that reminds you of the deep love you have inside to improve the quality of life on earth.

SCAN

You are now well prepared to scan your own or someone else's energy using the human energy system as a framework. Scanning is an intuitive, non-judgmental process in which you observe the flow of energy and assess where the areas of *surplus* and *deficiency* are located. The interpretation and evaluation can come later.

You can either scan the other person when he or she is present or imagine the person in front of you. Repeat his or her name either out loud or silently, and use the main place of residence as a focal point for their soul's energy home. Then scan the chakras one at a time and remember which one(s) is/are *asking* for the most attention.

Once your scan is complete, the personal energy tends to flow more freely because your positive intent already opens new pathways for healing. On a more advanced level, you can take classes and workshops on how to apply specific modalities to the chakra that you sense is out of balance, such as chakra hypnosis or sound healing. As a beginner, I recommend you simply place one or two hands over the energy center you address and repeat these words: *steady energy flow*. This will either calm or stimulate the chakra you focus on; whichever is appropriate.

Don't worry if you don't immediately get an intuitive impression the first time. Like everything else in life, practice makes perfect. With a little persistence you will soon pick up fluctuations and signals, maybe even messages in the form of words or phrases. If you have a talent for this, the results will come sooner and more pronounced. Over time you can develop your skill and perhaps become my student; I love teaching others to become healing facilitators. Since this is much more a lifestyle than a profession, I don't foresee myself ever retiring from educating others about the healing force.

Negative Places

Just as you may come across negative people that interfere with your intuitive perception and overall energy level, you may also find yourself in *negative places*. External energy interference can originate from other sources than human beings, although it is very possible that the *energy leak* or *block* is generated through man-made substances, objects, or equipment.

In our modern society we are surrounded by electronic equipment that produces electromagnetic frequencies (EMFs). Examples are power lines, home wiring, airport and military radar, substations, transformers, computers, and other appliances. Just like air pollution, *electrosmog* is an inseparable part of our modern day society and EMFs will continue to be around us. People who are interested in enhancing their intuitive perception often choose to *go green* and live more consciously. I recommend prudent avoidance of electromagnetic interference, where possible.

As part of my training as an energy healer I became certified in feng shui, the Oriental art of placement that helps us to live in harmony with our environment. When I conduct consultation visits in homes or places of business, I always do an environmental energy analysis. I use EMF measuring equipment, such as gigahertz and Gauss meters and thoroughly check each area for interference.

I also rely on my intuitive perception to detect lay lines or water veins in the earth, known as dowsing. If present, these natural pathways can block or accelerate the flow of energy and generate what is called *geopathic stress*.

Although specific protective measurements and clearing remedies may be necessary depending on the complexity of a particular environment, these are general guidelines by the Environmental Protection Agency (EPA) to minimize the negative effect of EMFs and electrosmog on your personal energy:

- Have your home, work or creative environment measured for Gauss levels. Avoid areas above 1mG.
- Don't let children play near power lines, transformers, radar domes, and microwave towers.
- If you choose to sleep under an electric blanket or on a waterbed, make sure you unplug them before going to bed.
- Rearrange your office and home area so that you are not exposed to EMFs from the sides or backs of electric appliances and computers. In the home, it is best that all major electrical appliances, such as computers, TVs, refrigerators etc, be placed up against outside walls. That way you are not creating an EMF field in the adjoining room.
- Don't sit too close too your computer.
- Don't stand close too your microwave oven.
- Avoid sleeping in a room where the power enters the home.
- Move all electrical appliances at least six feet from your bed. Eliminate wires running under your bed.
- Be wary of cordless appliances such as electric toothbrushes and razors.
- Decide not to wear a quartz watch because it radiates pulsating EMFs along your energy meridians.
- Wear as little jewelry as possible and to take it off at night; metal conducts electricity.

Trauma Places

Some environments have a collective traumatic history that influences the people who live and work there in the present time. I remember going to a home in Connecticut, where the EMFs and electrosmog checked out OK. The location of the home was very favorable with water views of the Long Island Sound. The home was well designed and tastefully decorated. Nevertheless, the residents, a couple, and their two children were all suffering from various chronic complaints such as migraine headaches, interrupted sleep, mood swings, low energy, and concentration problems. The family had a healthy lifestyle including good nutrition, exercise, and creative activities.

I suspected historic interference and decided to go into a deep meditation after creating a power shield with large crystals and other power objects in the center of the home. In trance, my mind was able to move into a dimension that revealed a clear picture of soldiers and minutemen fighting a battle on these grounds. In my vision, many men died and this traumatic event left a strong imprint on the energy of the property.

"So our house is haunted?" the lady of the house asked me. "Well, it really doesn't feel like that to me," I said. "My sense is that it's not the house but the grounds that are full of pain and suffering. I recommended doing a healing ceremony to honor those who fought and died for freedom and independence and to bless their spirits." After that, the energy changed dramatically and the family continued to live in their home with minimal health complaints.

Historic places of horrible trauma, such as World War II concentration camps, major battlefields, and the site in New York known as Ground Zero, should all be treated with the utmost caution. The shocked energy is very powerful and will continue to influence the energetic environment of the site for many ages.

Power Places

Fortunately, there are also many spots on planet Earth that are regarded as *power places*. These sites function as amplifiers of positive energy and we find them all over the world. There are many lists of seven wonders that are regarded by many as strengthening places because they are either awesome natural wonders or spectacular man-made structures.

Since 2007 there are *seven new wonders of construction*, although the Great Pyramids of Giza are there as an honorary eighth member and the only existing site of the *Seven Ancient Wonders of the World* list.

The new ones are:

- Great Wall (China)
- Petra (Jordan)
- Christ the Redeemer Statue (Brazil)
- Machu Picchu (Peru)
- Chichen Itza (Mexico)
- Colosseum (Italy)
- Taj Mahal (India)

Then there are the Seven *Natural* Wonders of the World:

- Grand Canyon (USA)
- Great Barrier Reef (Australia)
- Harbor of Rio de Janeiro
- Mount Everest (Nepal)
- Aurora Borealis (Polar Circle)
- Paricutin Volcano (Mexico)
- Victoria Falls (Zambia/Zimbabwe)

I have visited two of the sites on these lists, Machu Picchu and the Grand Canyon. Both experiences have had a profound influence on me. Being immersed in the energy of these power places signified a spiritual graduation for me. The first time I felt a similar feeling was when I visited Stonehenge at age eighteen, while doing a three-week bicycle tour in the south of England. This rite of passage was my introduction to Celtic mysticism and I found out that Great Britain has numerous power places like this, all well-indicated on the Ordinance Survey road maps.

Another very important place to amplify my intuition has been Sedona, Arizona. The red rock area in and around this town has a series of sites, called *vortexes*, where energy vibrations are higher and stronger. This automatically enhances one's intuitive perception. The collective consciousness of the many Native American cultures has made it an ideal spot for my spiritual retreats, mindfulness tours, and vision quests.

Intuitive Energy Healers

Intuitive energy healers tend to be private people with a strong sense of purpose and idealistic goals. We have a deep commitment to positivity and goodness and we often make big sacrifices to achieve our ideals. We are prone to errors of fact because we follow our feelings more than we follow logical analysis. However, we usually don't make errors of feeling.

Generally speaking, intuitive healers are introspective, cooperative, informative, and attentive. A calm and composed exterior may mask a passionate inner life. We care deeply about causes that interest us and we often pursue those causes with strong devotion. We value compassion and empathy and we seek to bring peace, health, and integrity to our companions and to society at-large. We want to heal the problems that trouble individuals and correct the conflicts that divide social groups.

Intuitive healers strive to develop adaptability, flexibility, and patience with complicated situations, and welcome new ideas and information. We are impatient with scientific details. Aware of people's feelings, intuitive healers relate well with others. Given our private nature, we are comfortable working by ourselves and we don't easily feel lonely. We have a keen interest in scholarly activities, especially relating to language.

We value harmony and integrity in human relationships, but we often find these values to be out of alignment with the material pursuits of others. Intuitive healers can easily feel isolated. Feeling *different,* we may sometimes wonder if something is wrong with our values. However, those differences often are our greatest strengths.

One of the most famous intuitive healers of the modern era was Edgar Cayce (1877-1945), a psychic healer and psychic trance channeler. Known as *the Sleeping Prophet*, he would lie down, enter a trance state, and then give his readings. It is reported that he gave about 20,000 readings in his lifetime. Cayce claimed to be a devout Christian albeit with beliefs outside of the norm. He was most famous for channeling answers to questions concerning the health of distant patients. There are numerous testimonials to the effectiveness of his distant healing diagnoses.

Medical Intuition

A *medical intuitive* is a health practitioner who uses his or her intuitive abilities to find the cause of a physical or emotional condition. A medical intuitive may determine areas of concern from a holistic point of view and recommend physical or psychological evaluation through a qualified health professional and give advice on general, nutritional or lifestyle changes. Medical intuitives may have a medical training but they do not make a formal medical diagnosis. The recommendations they give usually encourage people to be active participants in their healing process.

The practice of using intuition or clairvoyance for medical information dates back to Phineas Parkhurst Quimby, whose intuitive healing practice began in 1854. William M. Branham, the father of the Pentecostal Latter Rain Movement, was said by his followers to be able to discern the health condition of people that attended his services, and in many cases heal them of their affliction. The term medical intuitive was first introduced by neurosurgeon Norman Shealy, MD, PhD, along with Caroline Myss in 1987 as part of Dr. Shealy's research on intuition and medical application.

A medical intuition evaluation can provide invaluable information about issues of the physical body, but can also identify mental and emotional factors that act as direct contributors to health issues. Instead of labeling a disorder, a medical intuitive can identify the location of inflammation in the body, evaluate the health of a gland or organ, or validate a strong emotion that is impacting health. Many times, a medical intuitive can identify imbalances within the body long before it fully manifests as a disease.

I have been fortunate to have one of the most brilliant medical intuitives as my main mentor, Dr. Sonja de Graaff van Mastrigt. Her amazing abilities have inspired me to develop my own intuitive skills and move beyond my perceived limitations. Dr. Sonja has the innate ability to bring clarity and simplicity to complex health challenges. Combining a deep sense of compassion with advanced skills in integrative medicine, she has helped thousands of patients recover from serious illness. She has taught me the importance of prevention by identifying the underlying causal factors of disease.

Another notable author, teacher, and medical intuitive, Meredith L. Young-Sowers, has founded the Stillpoint Institute, of which I am a graduate and former adjunct teacher. My experience at Stillpoint has awakened my personal sense of spirituality and deepened my awareness of how spiritual energy moves with the mind and through the body.

Intuitive Self-Actualization

The process of self-actualization can be challenging but I have found that it is much easier if you engage your intuition. It will lead to a faster degree of self-improvement and ultimately to the success you desire. Your intuitive perception can help you see yourself from your highest point of view. Using the BLESS method on yourself will open your consciousness to a new vision for your life. Once you have your dreams, aspirations, and goals well imagined, you will be able to start creating and manifesting.

The next chapter explains the process of personal mind mapping, my method of organizing your intuitive information in a practical form. Using this method helps you to create an action plan for the various notions and ideas that come to your mind and makes it easy to focus on what is really important for you. After all, a goal without a *plan* is merely a daydream.

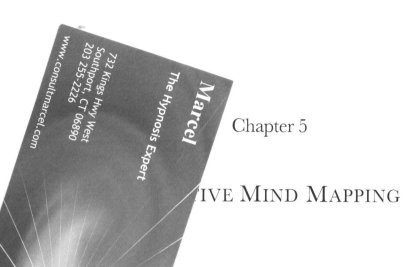

Chapter 5

IVE MIND MAPPING

imitations to the mind except those we acknowledge."

~ Napoleon Hill

Our ability to influence our mind depends a lot on our *intention*. How we are inspired and motivated by our inner and outer world causes either constructive or destructive effects for our mind's potential. Designing intent through *positive mind mapping* is a way of taking charge of your mind and creating an opportunity to live your life's purpose. Focused attention happens when you use *all* your senses, including intuition.

Positive mind mapping combines your own natural thinking with a powerful process that provides the universal key to unlock the dynamic potential of your mind. It is a highly effective way of getting information in and out of your conscious mind and linking it to the subconscious part of your mind. It is a creative and logical method of taking and making notes that literally *map out,* so that your mind's potential can expand without feeling overwhelmed. *It's not what you think, it's how you go with the flow.*

Attention

As a child I had difficulty being quiet, sitting still, and paying attention. Sometimes, my behavior was seen as precociously cute but more often it was regarded as disturbing and it often got me into trouble both at home and at school. This is illustrated in chapter one. My mind needed to release creative energy but had not yet learned what the consequences would be. My interpretation of the teacher's scolding words while making too much noise in her classroom was also creative but missed the point she was trying to make. I took her words literally and, as a consequence, I caused quite a stir.

These types of situations particularly happened when I sensed conflict or chaos. Most likely, I would have been diagnosed with attention deficit hyperactivity disorder (ADHD), if the term had already been invented.

These are the diagnostic criteria for ADHD:

- Often does not pay close attention to detail, or makes careless mistakes in schoolwork, work, or other activities
- Often has trouble focusing attention on tasks or play activities
- Often seems to not listen when spoken to directly
- Often does not follow instructions and fails to finish schoolwork, chores, or duties in the workplace (not due to oppositional behavior or failure to understand instructions)
- Often has trouble organizing activities
- Often avoids, dislikes, or doesn't want to do things that take a lot of mental effort for a long period (such as schoolwork or homework)
- Often loses things needed for tasks and activities (toys, school assignments, pencils, books, or tools)
- Is often easily distracted
- Is often forgetful in daily activities
- Often mixes up names of people or forgets them for short periods of time.

ADHD is categorized as a *disorder* and medical professionals will often prescribe stimulants, non-stimulants, anti-depressants, or even blood pressure medication to control the symptoms. However, these drugs can cause side effects such as loss of appetite, weight loss, sleep problems, irritability, tics, dry mouth, dizziness, upset stomach, and there are even concerns about suicidal thoughts. I am not opposed to conventional medicine but I prefer to use safe, non-invasive ways that can either prevent or remedy a health challenge. My favorite mottos are *Hugs before Drugs* and *Meditation before Medication*.

Chess

For the young Marcel, seven out of ten of the above-mentioned criteria would have applied but that does not mean that I was less able to master skills or perform creative tasks, I just needed a different approach. People with ADHD often have high IQs and can do extremely well in life provided that they can operate in a comfortable and supportive environment. They do not respond well to forceful pressure— it causes them to feel overwhelmed and they eventually withdraw. However, when you give them encouragement they will be able to channel their mental versatility to top levels.

At age eleven, I was an avid chess player and a member of our school team. My friends and I played the game every day and we competed a lot against other schools. Eventually we rose to fame by making it all the way to the national finals. Of course, I felt proud about this achievement but it never seemed like I had to struggle or sacrifice much to get to that level. After all, I was just having fun playing the game and I intuitively learned to figure out strategies to build strong positions on the chessboard.

Chess players usually have an analytical mind and often excel at math but that did not apply to me. Numbers did not interest me a whole lot at that age but I was still able to play very strongly and defeat many other kids and adults. The essence was that I played by *feel* and created routines and structures through repetition while feeling good. You could say I was *training my brain* while being *kind to my mind*. This is still my preferred way of learning.

Imagination

What I like most about people who have been labeled with ADHD is their powerful imagination, searching insight, and unusual intuition. To me these are the *gifted ones* that simply need to learn how to give proper attention to their uniqueness. When I grew up, I was fortunate to learn techniques that helped me use my abilities efficiently and grow into a happy adult. I decided to use my own imagination to create a program that can help the young ones and their parents.

Part of the program is based on my own tendency to *doodle*. A doodle is an unfocused drawing you make while your attention is occupied with something else. Doodles can either be simple drawings with a specific symbolic meaning or they can simply be abstract shapes. Like many students, I doodled a lot in my school notebooks while I was daydreaming or losing interest during class. Later on in life I produced many doodles during phone conversations.

Then, a study showing that doodling can help someone's memory caught my attention. It concluded that doodling generates just enough energy to keep a person from daydreaming, which demands a lot of the brain's processing power, as well as from not paying attention. Thus, it acts as a mediator between the spectrum of thinking too much or thinking too little and helps focus on the current situation. The study was done at the School of Psychology at the University of Plymouth. It reported that doodlers in his experiment recalled seven and a half out of sixteen pieces of information on average, 29% more than the average of 5.8 recalled by the control group made of non-doodlers.

When I examined my doodles more closely, I found that I usually started with one symbol and then worked my way into various directions but connected most of my pictures and lines to the central symbol. In other words, while in a daydreaming state I kept myself steady by staying connected to the main theme, very interesting. I was creating an organizational structure— a *mind map*— so I would not get lost.

Mapping the Mind

When I explored this creative process more, I discovered that other people had also come to the conclusion that this natural way for people to steady their mind can be taken to a higher level. Research shows that making mind maps encourages anyone to manage and process information and improve attention difficulties. It is a unique and noninvasive method to encourage people to simplify and make more sense of their world— whether it's an academic topic or a life skill, such as time management. It makes it an ideal tool in learning how to better manage your mind and create a more meaningful and purposeful life with less distractions and frustrations.

One simple way to understand a mind map is by comparing it to a map of a city. The city center represents the main idea. The main roads leading from the center represent the key thoughts in your thinking process. The secondary roads or branches represent your secondary thoughts, and so on. Special images or shapes can represent landmarks of interest or particularly relevant ideas.

Positive mind mapping can help children and adults in many ways:

- Planning
- Note taking
- Brainstorming
- Problem solving
- Stimulating creativity
- Presenting information
- Studying and memorization
- Gaining insight on complex subjects
- Researching and consolidating information

Just as in every great idea, the power lies in the simplicity. In a mind map, as opposed to traditional note taking or a linear text, information is structured in a way that resembles how your brain actually works. Since it is an activity that is both analytical and artistic, it engages your brain in a much richer way, helping in all its cognitive functions. It also has a high fun factor!

Creating a Mind Map

This is a very basic mind map about positive mind mapping itself. It pictures the core elements and techniques on how to draw mind maps.

I recommend you use many colors and different symbols to make the mind map as visual as possible. Keep your topic labels to *one single word* or *one picture* and vary the size of your text and thickness of the lines as much as possible. This helps to engage the brain part of your mind more.

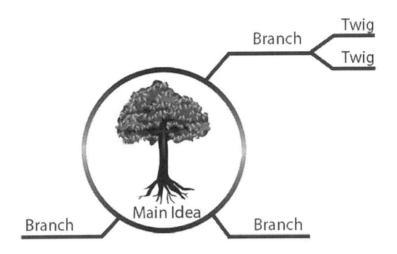

Drawing your own mind map is really simple:

- Start in the middle of a blank page, writing or drawing the idea you intend to develop
- Draw the related subtopics around this central topic, connecting each of them to the center with a line
- Repeat the same process for the subtopics, drawing lower-level subtopics if you want, connecting each of those to the corresponding subtopic.

Remember that the brain is only *part* of the mind. We know that it is an important switchboard for the mind and mapping out ideas is therefore an important component of my positive mind mapping program. The inspiration and motivation to work out an idea lies at the foundation for a new direction for your life. After the organizational part, your plan needs to be put into action. To implement or execute your vision, another type of energy is necessary, called *determination*. Here is a success story of how positive mind mapping, in combination with hypnosis, has worked for a medical student.

Angelique's Story

When Angelique called me she was in a state of panic and she sounded as if the house was on fire! Time to apply some emergency phone hypnosis. "Angelique," I said. "Listen to my voice, remember? Just listen to my voice. I'm right here. Everything's going to be fine. Take a deep breath. Good. Once more, deep breathe. All right. Now say: I'm calm, relaxed and in control. Very good. Now do that again. Deep breath. I'm calm, relaxed, and in control. Excellent. Now keep breathing slowly and tell me what's the matter. "I cannot do this," she said. "There's just not enough time. It's all way too much, too much work. This was not a good idea!"

A week before, Angelique had come in for a positive mind mapping program with me. She was very excited about a new goal in her life: passing the US Medical Board Exam. This was certainly not an easy task, especially because there was only limited time to prepare, but she sounded enthusiastic and determined about it. After all, she had obtained her medical degree in Europe fifteen years earlier and she had been a successful researcher and practitioner ever since. Angelique asked me to help her keep a focused mind while going through the study books.

She was familiar with the power of the mind and she had studied hypnosis in the past. She loved listening to guided imagery tapes but admitted falling asleep easily when the progressive relaxation took too long. I suggested using a rapid hypnotic induction method to make sure she would not go to sleep, but stay in trance while I kept giving her positive suggestions. Angelique responded very well and reported improvements after each follow-up session. She was really enjoying refreshing her knowledge while going through the first few books.

As new books on anatomy and physiology came in the mail, Angelique's analytical mind started thinking, "What am I doing? I only have four more months to refresh the detailed information that medical students normally take four *years* to absorb!" Mind mapping helped her to organize her thoughts, get back on track, and feel good about her original plan. However, as books on gynaecology and surgery arrived, Angelique became quite restless and could not fall asleep at night. Hypnosis helped her get into a sound and restful sleep and awaken refreshed, renewed, and full of positive energy.

Even though this kept her steady, she could not stop wondering if it might have been better to temporarily close her practice. When she finally received the pharmacology books, it was as if her rational mind short-circuited. Fortunately, her subconscious remembered the phrase I tend to say to clients when they leave my office "Call me when you need me." My voice helped her to calm down and soon she felt steady and at ease again.

We decided to design a special plan of action that would bypass all the new knowledge her conscious mind thought she needed to learn. Instead, we would give her mind permission to rely completely on the knowledge and experience stored in her subconscious memory banks. In other words, there really was no need for her to study anymore, other than for the latest updates in pharmacology. All the answers were already in her permanent memory archives, neatly structured as mind maps, when she went through it years earlier. She really liked that suggestion. The pressure of all that studying and memorizing was simply too stressful, but with the proper hypnotic techniques and reinforcement she knew this was going to work!

I realized that the suggestions would have to be specific enough to apply to the different exams. I had no clear idea of how to do that yet, but I trusted my intuition to come up with something in time. I learned that the medical board exam is quite an intense event during which complete nervous breakdowns are not uncommon in students.

In the hypnosis session two weeks before the board exam, Angelique imagined stepping into a magnificent library. Here her passion for reading books was symbolized by a warm glow she would feel each time she placed one hand over her heart. The glow would spread throughout her body, keeping her calm and relaxed with each question of the exam. Then, her mind would use the appropriate map to find the applicable book on the shelf. It would open at the appropriate page and all she had to do was use that knowledge to give the correct answer. As a hypnotist, I like to go into a light trance myself when helping a client. It enhances my focus and ability to tap into my own mind map library. The imagery in these sessions was so vivid that at times I believed I could take the exam myself!

A week before the exams, Angelique felt confident enough to go into the exams and make it through the week all right. However, she was concerned that something would cause her mind library to be closed. I offered to meet her every day at the exam building and do a fifteen-minute hypnosis session specifically for the exams of that day. I also gave her a card with a special post-hypnotic suggestion for multiple-choice questions. The phrase was, "Only one of these answers is right. It will glow when you say the word *light*." The idea was to imagine the correct answer to appear highlighted on the page. Angelique was already in the habit of highlighting sentences in books, so she connected very well with this suggestion.

On the first day of the board exams we were both very calm, relaxed, and in control. We found a private room and during the short hypnotic induction a new suggestion came to me. I told Angelique she would stay in a *light trance* all throughout the exams of the day. This way, she would not be bothered by whatever went on around her. She would not even feel hungry, but she would continue to drink plenty of water and take regular walks to keep the circulation going. She called me at 5:00 p.m. and she told me it went phenomenally well! Not only was she able to apply all suggestions, the day also appeared to have flown by and she did not feel exhausted at all. It was funny to hear that she did feel rather hungry, because we included a time frame for the suggestion only until 5:00 p.m. I made sure to include a modified appetite suggestion the next day.

Each of the other exam days went similarly for Angelique. In the morning, I showed up for a short session and the rest was up to her. At the end of the week she just *knew* she had done really well. A few weeks later, the letter with her exam results came in. Her score was the highest score ever recorded! When she told me the good news, I was elated. We congratulated each other and felt proud and excited about this achievement. Today, Angelique continues her healing work even more successfully. She frequently recommends my positive mind mapping program to her patients for healing and self-improvement.

Personality

In my work as a healer, as well as in my personal life, I have met many people with a variety of backgrounds and social status. Each of them has a different DNA and a personal uniqueness that may enable them to find an authentic purpose in life. Often they are looking for direction and guidance because they have overemphasized a certain aspect of their personality. Usually, one part of them has become dominant and prefers a specific environment or *comfort zone*.

Depending on which side of our personality we present the most, our mind maps move in the direction of either an *extravert* or *introvert*. These terms were first popularized by Carl Jung's analytical psychology. Extravert means *outward-turning* and introvert means *inward-turning*. The preferences for extraversion and introversion are known as *attitudes*. Each of the cognitive functions can operate in the external world of behavior, action, people, and things (*extraverted attitude*) or the internal world of ideas and reflection (*introverted attitude*).

The Extravert

Extraverts tend to enjoy human interactions and are usually enthusiastic, talkative, assertive, and gregarious. They take pleasure in activities that involve large social gatherings like parties, community activities, public demonstrations, and business or political groups. Politics, teaching, sales, managing, and brokering are fields that favor extraversion. Extraverts tend to be energized when they are around other people and more prone to boredom when they are on their own.

Extraverts, on the inside, are fluid. They have a flexible sense of who they are. They tend to change, based on their mood and their circumstances. With this fluidness comes the ability to enjoy variety in areas such travel, trying different things and foods, as well as a general sense of wanting to experience all aspects of life.

Extraverts don't want to miss out on anything in life. Because they don't have a rigid sense of self, they sometimes doubt their own abilities, needing encouragement and validation from other people they trust. They are more dependent in their external environment for validation of their self-worth. Because extraverts tend to doubt themselves a lot, what they dislike the most is to be *ignored*. When they are or feel ignored, it feels lonely, and they question themselves. They need reinforcement that they are doing a good job or are wanted and loved. In leadership positions, extraverts surround themselves with people who will encourage them when they take risks.

The Introvert

Introverts have a solid sense of who they are. They tend to be very self-sufficient. If they are challenged or overwhelmed, they tend to pull back. They then can slip in feeling self-righteous because they are pretty sure they *know* what is going on and they feel they understand the situation.

Introverts are people whose energy expands through reflection and meditation. They are more reserved and less outspoken in large groups. They tend to enjoy solitary activities such as reading, writing, music, drawing, watching movies and plays, and spending time behind a computer. In fact, social networking sites have become a home-away-from-home for introverts in the twenty-first century. On Facebook, Twitter, MySpace, LinkedIn and so forth, the formalities of social conduct are bypassed and the introvert can become more comfortable blogging about personal circumstances and feelings they would not talk about in direct interactions with people

Introverts are not necessarily *shy*. Shy people avoid social encounters, whereas the introvert just prefers solitary activities to social ones. For introverts, *trust* is very important, especially in forming relationships. They prefer to concentrate on a single person or activity at a time and like to observe someone or some situations before they participate. Introverts are easily *overwhelmed* by too much stimulation from social gatherings and engagement and think things through before they express their opinion.

The Ambivert

If you are wondering whether you are an extravert or an introvert, it is possible that you may be both. About 85 percent of people are *ambivert*, both extroverted and introverted, but not necessarily in equal proportions. An ambivert is normally comfortable with groups and enjoys social interaction but also enjoys time alone, away from crowds. An ambivert may be more introverted under some circumstances and more extraverted in other situations.

For healers, counselors, therapists, and social workers in general it would be best to cultivate ambiversion. In any type of helping capacity it is important to create rapport and be able to help the other person feel understood. In my work it is very useful to know how to shift from serene to enthusiastic, depending on the other person's personality and the individual mind maps they focus on.

A Mind of Our Own

All our human minds have many things in common. However, we create *a mind of our own* as it forms and shapes with experiences. Even if it were legally and ethically possible to clone a human being, the identical DNA would not produce the same person with the same mindset. Our personality, maturity, and wisdom develop over time depending on the internal and external programming. How each individual operates is the result of a complex matrix of thoughts, feeling, and subtle energy.

My passion for music is tremendously fulfilling to me. It enables me to express both my extravert and introvert qualities, with songwriting on the one side and performing a show on the other side. It is because of positive mind mapping that I have been able to channel my mind's potential into creative end products that I can share with others. Music can generate powerful healing energy. It can soothe the soul, comfort the heart, and bring peace of mind. In the next chapter I will tell you how I use this part of my authentic self to facilitate healing and bring harmony in my own life and that of others.

Chapter 6

THE HEALING POWER
OF SOUND AND MUSIC

"Music gives a soul to the universe, wings to the mind,
flight to the imagination, and life to everything."

~ Plato

Life's Soundtrack

In chapter one, I mentioned that I have always loved people, probably from the day I was born. It is very possible that I have loved *music* even from before my date of birth. As I grew up, my love for music became a passion and an increasing amount of songs became part of the soundtrack of my life. This process continued as my life evolved. It has resulted in an expanding variety of musical projects that all symbolize life experiences or phases I go through. I enjoy the process of creating music that captures the essence of healing. Therefore, hearing how my compositions positively affect other people's lives is tremendously satisfying for me.

All members of my family loved music. My mother played piano and my father played the clarinet. My two older brothers owned a lot of records so I had access to a large variety of musical genres. After starting to play guitar at age eleven, I gradually learned how to sing and strum simultaneously. The first song I wrote was well received at a school performance and I felt encouraged to continue exploring my passion. Throughout my college years I played in a rock/pop band called Pixwart. It was an exciting time and we were quite popular as a support act for well-known, successful bands. This also gave me the opportunity to observe up-close what goes on behind the scenes of fame and celebrity— some of it was fun but a lot of it was not pretty.

Fortunately, I had already embarked on a path of health and wellness and I had discovered that smoking, doing drugs, and heavy drinking were not part of the lifestyle I wanted. I enjoyed being onstage and interacting with an audience but after a while the rock music scene did not appeal to me anymore. I decided to shift to recording projects that were more in line with the energy of healing and joy.

In my healing work, I like to have calming, soothing background music playing. It supports me in *setting the tone* and it helps me to focus my mind better, so I can give my client my full attention. With this in mind, Dr. Sonja and I got together to compose and record music that would support people in their healing process. We had been working together in several healing practices and this new endeavor, called Inner Healing Series, first resulted in the CD *Meditation Music for Someone Special*. This album has become a favorite of energy healers, massage therapists, hypnosis specialists, yoga instructors, and many others.

After this, we recorded our popular guitar album *Daydreams* and the CD *Happy Songs*, written to help kids in their healing with positivity and joy. The album is also appropriate for the inner child in each adult's heart. We perform at various children's hospitals helping children to find joy and expression in their challenges. We have also produced ten different guided imagery CDs that each concentrate on a specific aspect of healing through spoken word and music. They have been enormously helpful to many people in a variety of ways: deep relaxation, stress management, weight control, immune system support, pain control, exercise motivation, forgiveness healing, and self-esteem.

Two of these recordings, *Deep Relaxation* and *Protected by the Light*, have been used in Dr. Sonja's 2001 double-blind research study at Yale New

Haven hospital on breast cancer patients. I was personally involved as a research assistant and offered to help in any way I could. My mother had died of breast cancer in 1989 and Dr. Sonja had been diagnosed with the disease in 1994 so I was extra motivated to help this research project succeed. The end report was regarded as *outstanding* and has contributed to an increased awareness of the healing capacity of voice and music.

My latest album is called *Soulmates*, which features a selection of original songs that focus on spiritual connections and energy exchanges. The power of music and lyrics can move people into healing their mind and body. Sometimes our emotional state needs a serious musical piece, sometimes a lighthearted song. I love exploring all aspects of healing through music. You can see a complete overview of all my original compositions at the end of this book (Appendix).

Sound Healing

The sound of a particular song can cause you to vividly remember experiences that you had at the time you first heard that music. As a result, you may not only hum or sing along with a song, but momentarily feel like a teenager again if the tune is from that phase of your life. As a musician, this phenomenon continues to fascinate me. As a healer I have always looked for ways to incorporate musicality in my practice. Many of my clients have experienced amazing healing effects using *Sound Healing*. I use various musical tools to positively influence the vitality of organs and tissues. In these sessions we use special instruments that create healing vibrations, such as *Himalayan bowls*. My set of singing bowls is very precious to me and they are my preferred music tools to tune and align subtle energy fields.

Some instruments I use, such as *tingshaws* or temple bells, produce ultra low frequency (ULF) sounds. These sounds have the capacity to speed up physical and emotional healing and have helped improve the following health issues: fears, anger, stress, injuries, fatigue, circulation, indigestion, congestion, blood pressure, muscle tension, sexual problems, and sleep difficulties. The Native American flute enhances breath awareness and various drums bring stimulation and motivation to people's energy when they feeling sluggish or stuck.

For many years I have used an exciting healing tool to balance a person's vibrational frequencies. It is called the TranceMaster and it combines the rhythm, pitch, and musical effect of sound with light stimulation. It has been particularly effective for improving memory and learning skills. It also has an amazing healing effect on ADHD and can work wonders for motivation, especially when combined with hypnotic suggestions.

Another sound wave device I use applies sound frequencies to a revolutionary system of neurological, soft tissue reflexes that helps to resolve chronic and acute pain. The great thing about these technologies is that they are safe, non-invasive, and do not produce extra heat or pressure.

Musical Medicine

The intellectual and spiritual godfather of sound medicine was Pythagoras, the Greek philosopher and mathematician (580 – 500 BCE). Pythagoras is credited as the first person to take an organized approach to music as a healing technique. He called his method *musical medicine*. In the spring he would sit surrounded by his disciples who sang melodies accompanied by a lyre. They would sing chants in unison and the melodious and rhythmical patterns made them feel uplifted and enthusiastic about life. At other times, his disciples also used music as medicine. Certain melodies were composed to *cure* mental anguish. In addition, there were other melodies for anger, aggression, and for all psychological disturbances.

The human mind has not drastically changed since these times and the principles of sound healing apply perfectly to our modern-day life. Over the past twenty-five years, scientific research has provided a large amount of data on how sound and music is processed in the brain. Nowadays, functional magnetic resonance imaging (fMRI) has taught us about the neural connections of music. For many years researchers believed that the arts are processed in the right hemisphere of the brain while language and mathematics are processed in the left. We now know that processing music happens throughout nearly every region of the brain and its neural subsystems. Listening to music appears to activate areas of the brain that also process speech. One of our most important tools for healing is our spoken word— next to our positive intent— so it makes sense to use music, at least as a support to our vocabulary.

When a child is born, one of the most important signs of life is the breath. It's an instinctual response, of both infant and parents, to communicate. In the womb, a baby is already aware of sound, because the ear is fully developed three months after conception. Don Campbell, author of the popular book *The Mozart Effect*, cites several studies on the effects of music on the unborn child. The most important sound the fetus hears is its mother's voice. For this reason, it is recommended that the mother read to her unborn child. Rock music has been shown to drive the fetus to excessive kicking and even violent movements when played to the unborn. In contrast, Mozart and Vivaldi are most pleasing to the child, particularly Mozart's violin concertos. In traditional Japanese culture, embryonic education is called *Tai-Kwo*, a philosophy that calls for the education of the child to start very early in a pregnancy.

New research in the fields of neuroscience and cognitive science regarding the effects of music on intelligence and learning shows that music facilitates language development and enhances creative expression in children.

Extensive research on the biological roots of music have resulted in the following conclusions:

- Music is universal. Studies on the effects of classical music and intelligence have produced the same favorable results in a variety of cultures
- Musical behaviors emerge in infancy. Children begin singing very early in life, often earlier than speech development
- Teaching children to play music exercises the brain, the sensory, cognitive, and perceptual system
- A strong music curriculum improves reading comprehension
- Dramatic, long-lasting effects of music and intelligence are more pronounced when there is instruction in music.

Animal studies show that constant exposure to chaotic, distorted music negatively alters the brain's structure. Even plants seem to abhor this type of music. Ivy growing on a home where classical music was played all day long flourished better than that on a house where occupants blasted heavy metal music.

Tone of Voice

Whether we are musically trained or not, most of us become expert listeners by the age of six. By this age we have internalized the basis of our ability to enjoy and appreciate music. We are hard-wired to derive pleasure from music and it is known as one of life's greatest and oldest delights. Because music shares many similarities with speech in how it is processed in our neural pathways, musical tunes and harmonic sounds can offer tremendous possibilities for healing and happiness.

We know from the communication pie chart below, as taught in neuro-linguistic programming (NLP) training, that in a conversation or presentation the importance of words (verbal) is only 7%. The tonality (vocal) takes up 38% and body language (visual) is even more important with 55%. Since most clients have their eyes closed when they are in a hypnotic state, the tone of voice becomes the powerful vehicle to deliver the message of positive change. Thus, a monotone voice may not be the best one to use in presentations. In most situations I recommend a more enthusiastic, even melodious voice.

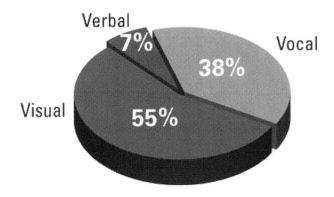

Tonality is extremely important in healing sessions. With the right inflection of words the human voice can promote relaxation, tranquility, optimism, motivation, enthusiasm, compassion, and love. When I do a review hypnosis session and guide someone back to his or her childhood, I sometimes softly sing "Happy Birthday To You" and the effects are amazing! That song can bring up all types of images of sensitizing events— either positive or negative— and can initiate deeper healing.

Entrainment

Even in an initial meeting with a person you can set the tone of the conversation by resonating with their tonality first and then subtly shifting into a different tone of voice. This is a form of what is called *entrainment*. Entrainment is a principle of physics, defined as the synchronization of two or more rhythmic cycles. Dutch physicist Christiaan Huygens was the first one to observe this phenomenon in 1665. While working on the design of the pendulum clock, Huygens found that if he placed two unsynchronized clocks side by side on a wall, their swings would slowly synchronize to each other. In fact, the synchronization was so precise not even mechanical intervention could calibrate them more accurately. A clock is a simple example of a system responding to entrainment, but the same rules apply to more complex systems such as the human brain.

Entrainment is actually an aspect of *resonance*. Resonance may be defined as the frequency at which an object most naturally wants to vibrate. One object may set another object into motion if it shares the same resonant frequency. If, for example, you strike a tuning fork of one hundred cycles per second and bring it near another tuning fork of that same frequency, the second tuning fork will be set in motion. Even though it has not been struck, the second fork will begin to vibrate and sound merely by being in the same field as the vibrating tuning fork.

You may have seen a singer break a glass with his or her voice. This is another example of resonance. This also occurs between two guitar strings, one struck and one unstruck. With resonance you are meeting the natural vibrations of an object with its own vibrations and thereby setting it into motion. When you slow down your breath, you slow down your heartbeat and your brain waves. Conversely, if you are able to slow down your brain waves, you can affect your heart rate and respiration. The frequencies of pulse, breathing, and blood circulation, as well as their combined activities, all function harmonically.

We find entrainment throughout nature. Fireflies blinking on and off entrain with each other. Female college roommates often have menstrual cycles that synchronize together. Muscle cells from the heart, when they move closer together, suddenly shift in their rhythm and start pulsing together, perfectly synchronized. This entrainment also takes place when two people have a good conversation. Their brain waves are in sync.

Musical Grammar

What we actually hear comes at the end of a long chain of mental processes that lead to an impression or mental image of the physical world. Our brain learns a certain *musical grammar* and our ability to make sense out of music is based on experience and neural structures that can learn and change every time we hear a new piece of music. In this way, we develop emotional changes, depending on the sort of music that is entering our perception, as follows:

Soft, melodic music
- Improves mood and relaxation
- Ideal for studying abstract concepts

Loud, strong rhythmic music
- Energizing
- Encourages motion such as aerobics and dancing

Waltz music
- Soothing, reduces stress
- Encourages slow dancing

Jazz music
- Sets a romantic mood
- Encourages lingering over a meal

Classical music
- Improves concentration
- Enhances learning when used as background music

Rock music
- Encourages movement
- Increases energy and confidence

During the past decade, neuroscientists have discovered the strong connection between the brain's memory and emotional systems. The *amygdala*, considered to be the seat of human emotion, is located next to the *hippocampus*, the area involved in memory storage and retrieval. Neuro-imaging studies show that the amygdala is activated in reaction to music, but not to random sounds. Therefore, it is important to use a musical pattern in your voice and use it as a fragment similar to a radio *jingle* of about fifteen to thirty seconds— the capacity of auditory short-term memory.

After helping my client get into a meditative state for healing, I suggest this jingle to be programmed in *continuous loop* mode, in the same way as a favorite tune can repeat in ones head all day long. You can use one of your favorite songs or you can make up a song by using an affirmation and adding some tonality, either new or borrowed, from another song. Examples are:

- *We're happy together . . .* (The Turtles)
- *Take it easy, take it easy . . .* (The Eagles)
- *It's getting better all the time . . .* (The Beatles)
- *What a wonderful world . . .* (Louis Armstrong)
- *I feel good. I knew that I would, yeah . . .* (James Brown)
- *I've got sunshine on a cloudy day . . .* (The Temptations)
- *I will survive, I will survive, hey hey . . .* (Gloria Gaynor)

Brainwaves

In the study of mental states through the electroencephalogram, neurologists have characterized these five different states or types of waveforms:

Gamma	31+ Hertz	Hyper-alert
Beta	13 - 30+ Hertz	Awake and alert
Alpha	8 - 12 Hertz	Relaxed
Theta	3 - 7 Hertz	Reverie, Imagery, Near Sleep
Delta	0.5 - 2 Hertz	Sleep

Research, using brain scans, shows that it is almost impossible to tell from the reading whether a person is listening to music or imagining the music, because the brain waves are virtually identical. This is important information for healing because it suggests that, in listening to music, people use the same brain areas for remembering as for perceiving. The jingle you install becomes a repetitive suggestion attached to healing.

One of my clients uses a *tap spot* on the palm of his hand to control the volume and boosts it when he needs it. He remembers the song in his mind, turns it up, and then perceives himself the way he chooses to. He calls it his *personal tune-up* and it works like a charm for him

Vibration

Consider the fact that sound is *vibration* and everything creates vibration. In fact, the entire universe is in a state of vibration and each thing generates its own frequency that is unique. Also keep in mind that an adult human body contains an average of 70% water (for babies it is even 90%) and you will understand how important this information is for you and me. According to Japanese researcher Masaru, author of *The Hidden Messages in Water*, each time we send or receive a positive or negative vibe or intent, the fluids in our body (blood, lymph etc.) translate that message and will either align or become distorted.

Mitchell Gaynor, MD, a leading oncologist in New York, describes in his book *Sounds of Healing* potent ways to help his patients become cancer-free using sound, voice, and music. "If we accept that sound is vibration, and we know that vibration touches every part of our physical being, then we understand that sound is 'heard,' not only through our ears but through every cell in our body," writes Gaynor, who reminds us that the human body is at least 70 percent water— the perfect medium for carrying sound.

Chakra Toning

As a healer and musician I have an excellent opportunity to weave the wisdom of music into mind images and create a comfortable auditory blanket for my clients. Songs can be used as activators for their new subconscious program by tuning in to musical imagery and promoting *sound health*.

As we use our voice to make sounds, we produce either consonants or vowels. Consonants partially block or change the sound energy, whereas vowels are the "soul" of the sound that can result in *overtones*. These are the hidden vibrations that give the sound its energy and resonance. Author and teacher, Don Campbell, writes in his book *The Roar of Silence*, "The making of a vowel and overtone sound for three to five minutes brings a sense of well-being and balance to the body.

When this is done with no stress or tension in the jaw, skin temperature generally rises and the mind calms. As the specific epicenters of sound and pitch are studied and determined for each individual, it will become possible to stimulate the body internally through toning."

Below is a simple but powerful *chakra toning* exercise that I have introduced to many individuals and groups. It follows the chakra system and can create *harmony through humming and hissing*. I have received great feedback (pun intended) about the wonderful response people get when they express their energy this way. Through the power of our own vocal sounds we can allow ourselves to get in touch with inner frequencies, thereby releasing suppressed feelings and emotional energy.

Because without breath we cannot produce vocals, it is important to always start with a breathing exercise to open up the respiratory system and warm up the muscles of inhalation. The *breath of life* method described in chapter one is easy and very effective for this. Make sure you focus on expanding your belly with each in-breath to engage the largest muscle inhalation, the diaphragm. This also massages many of your internal organs and causes a relaxation response.

Now you are ready to use the following chart to produce the various sounds that resonate with each chakra. I recommend starting from the root chakra up and when you reach the crown chakra, you may either stop there or go back to the root chakra in reverse. You may want to find a place where you can practice undisturbed, such as in your car with the windows up. Not every passer-by would understand you are actually doing a harmonizing exercise and some people might be alarmed! Nevertheless, the effects of this practice are awesome— feeling is believing.

Chakra Toning Sounds

	Crown	SSS/FFF (whisper)
	Brow	EEE (me)
	Throat	Aye (say)
	Heart	AH (ma)
	Solar Plexus	OH (go)
	Sacral	OOO (you)
	Root	UHH (cup)

Signature Sound

When you practice chakra toning regularly, you will discover that a particular sound you produce affects you in a stronger way than others do. The specific characteristics of this sound are an expression of your personal wave patterns. We can call this your *signature sound*. The unique way in which you use vibrations creates a frequency that can positively influence your mind and body as well as that of others. You don't have to be a well-trained singer to produce this sound. It can be soft or loud, volume doesn't matter, but it is important that the sound feels good. By intuitively tuning in, I have created a large variety of signature sounds for numerous people to help them continue the healing process in their daily life.

With daily practice you become more familiar with your signature sound and it will gradually promote communication, creative expression, and self-confidence. This sonic autograph is very helpful to resolve conflicts in relationships as it brings calmness between people. Your signature sound can be regarded as a *sonic fingerprint* and no two people are alike. Your thoughts, emotions, and all body systems have their own frequencies that contribute to the total vibrational essence that you are.

Music and sound are powerful tools for restoring the inner harmony of the body and awakening the spirit. When you hear or feel a sound, it is not what you think that affects you. Understanding how and why the energy of sound and music influences us, without any thought involved, is essential for healing. Applying the musical principles of entrainment, resonance, toning, and harmonics can help us achieve overall wellness, greater vitality, and a deep level of fulfillment.

The sound of your authentic voice can move energy in a heartbeat. Combining this sound with an affirmation, a positive statement can serve as a wake-up call to rapidly shift your emotions and your behavior in the direction you choose. I have designed a special method to create this *AHA* feeling and the next chapter will explain in detail how everyone has the potential to instantly create a happy mind.

Chapter 7

A Happy Mind in Seven Seconds

"What is the meaning of life? To be happy and useful."

~ Tenzin Gyatso, the 14th Dalai Lama

Happiness

When I ask my friends, colleagues, or clients what it is they want in their life, they often reply, "I just want to be happy." Happiness seems to be an important goal but if you consider the goal of happiness thoroughly, it's not what you think. Constant happiness is not the goal, rather a side effect of *pursuing* your goals. If you were to be happy all the time you would not care about destruction, disaster, or disease. You would smile at abuse, aggression, and aggravation and you would stay overjoyed when struck by trouble, terror, or tragedy.

If we were continuously happy it would go against our soul's purpose to learn about our uniqueness and be useful to others in the process. *Not* feeling happy motivates us to strive, to improve, to grow, to invent, and to discover. As a result of this, we can experience many moments of happiness. These meaningful temporary states are powerful enough to recharge our energy for some time and live a content life in between those peak experiences.

Unhappiness appears to be easier to attain than happiness. Happiness requires awareness of things to be happy about. Because our mind seems to gear toward negative feelings more easily than to positive ones, we need constant reminders of all things beautiful, wonderful, delicious, exciting, joyful, pleasant, or simply good. There are plenty of opportunities to tap into this energy but we tend to get sidetracked by negativity. I have found that the human mind has the ability to practice happiness and become skilled in it. To make that process easier, I have developed an instant technique called the *AHA method*, which I will describe in this chapter.

Affirmations

After reading Louise Hay's book *You Can Heal Your Life* for the first time in 1984, my mind opened up to a new belief. I was about to embark on a new journey and her "List of Affirmations" became an important frame of reference for my life and my work as a healer. These affirmations are carefully formatted statements that should be repeated frequently.

For an affirmation to be effective, it needs to be present tense, positive, personal, and specific. Louise's affirmations are designed to help you re-program your thought patterns. By using them properly, the harmful or negative underlying belief that is psychologically supporting the illness can be replaced with a healing, positive belief, thereby removing an obstruction to healing.

As I became more familiar with the healing power of the mind, I used many different affirmations in my work with clients as well as for myself. I discovered that affirmations can work for you *if* you use them in the correct way. They are designed to clear the path to heal illnesses or other life's challenges. From there you can move onward and upward in life with focused attention. People often believe that through repeating affirmations, the manifestation of their dream will follow. This is not always how it works. The positive intent by itself will usually not create the end result you desire; it works much better to develop a plan and then implement it. The keyword for achieving success is *action*.

Motivation

Even though deliberate change starts with a thought, putting your intent into effect is a matter of movement. Before you can take action you need *motivation*, which means, you need to feel *moved* so you can put your *emotion in motion.* In other words, happiness is a result of consciously and subconsciously moving your flow of enthusiastic energy that stimulates you to feel joy. This can play out in various parts of your life and create or promote what I have called the Seven Healing Principles of Awareness. They give you insight on how to shift from an immobile thought to a mobile flow of energy. In essence they are connected to your subtle energy system and follow the spiritual values of each chakra.

The Seven Healing Principles of Awareness are:

1. Group Awareness
    It's not what you think . . .
    It's how you respond to others (Grounding/Sharing)

2. Creative Awareness
    It's not what you think . . .
    It's how you let inspiration flow (Creativity/Celebration)

3. Emotional Awareness
    It's not what you think . . .
    It's how you move your feelings (Self-Esteem/Presence)

4. Relationship Awareness
    It's not what you think . . .
    It's how you connect from your heart (Love/Compassion)

5. Self-Awareness
    It's not what you think . . .
    It's how you choose what you believe (Truth/Will)

6. Success Awareness
    It's not what you think . . .
    It's how you put your plan into action (Vision/Mission)

7. Spiritual Awareness
    It's not what you think . . .
    It's how you make a higher link (Universal Connection)

Healing Questions

When you apply these principles to your life, you can begin to realize that *thinking* by itself does not lead to healing. The awareness that follows the thought will guide you in a healing direction and give you choices to achieve happiness. In that process it is important to ask yourself the right questions. Healing questions are those that will lead you to a solution for your challenge or a resolution for your problem. They help you to take the high road to health and happiness.

Questions that will help you heal:

- *In what way can I help?*
- *What are the possibilities?*
- *What is my responsibility?*
- *How can I find a solution?*
- *Wouldn't it be great if . . . ?*
- *What can I learn from this?*
- *What is the best action I can take?*

Negative, blaming, or judging questions, on the other hand, will make you feel *stuck*. It is the inner critic at work, either toward yourself or others, and it causes you to go backwards or around in circles, resulting in limitation, inflexibility, or pessimism. These forms of stagnation can even lead to physical symptoms, such as migraine headaches, sinus congestion, tightness in the throat and chest, constipation, painful joints, and back problems.

Questions that will not help you heal:

- *Who is at fault?*
- *Who is to blame?*
- *Why even bother?*
- *What is wrong here?*
- *Why do I keep trying?*
- *What if this won't work?*
- *Why does this always happen to me?*

Creating optimism starts with asking healing questions. A happy mindset can eventually results from this. With this in mind, I developed a fine-tuning method that speeds up the process significantly.

Seven-Second Shift

In his book *You Are the Message: Secrets of the Master Communicators* Roger Ailes, president of Fox News Channel and media consultant for various former presidents, famously said: "You have just seven seconds to make a good first impression. The assessment of you that's formed in the first seven seconds creates a lasting impression of you in another's mind." It means that when you communicate with someone, it is not just the words you choose to send to the other person that make up the message.

You are also sending signals about what kind of person you are by your eyes, your facial expression, your body movement, your vocal pitch, tone, volume, and intensity, your commitment to your message, your sense of humor, and many other factors. The total of you affects how others think of and respond to you.

In my experience, this principle also applies to the way in which you perceive yourself. The communication that takes place within the conscious and subconscious part of the mind first opens a *thought field*. Within the next seven seconds it finds its way into the feeling part of your mind, through which you experience sensations that are translated in either a negative, positive, or neutral response.

I came to the realization that people can use this to create an *instantaneous* positive mind shift. Something that is profound but simple enough to easily remember and apply to any situation where someone wants to take charge of his or her mind. All you need is some basic instructions and a quick-reference list with abbreviated affirmations.

Automatic Happy Attitude

Sometimes people have a moment of sudden clarity known as *the aha! effect*. This refers to the common human experience of suddenly understanding a previously incomprehensible problem or concept. All at once you get it! It seems a switch is turned on in the brain that sheds a whole new light on the matter. It is mostly regarded as a positive thing because it enables a person to put a situation into perspective.

An *Automatic Happy Attitude* (AHA) is just that, a mood-enhancing clarifier that helps you to rapidly shift your feelings into positivity. There is a difference between a regular affirmation and an AHA. Affirmations tend to be one or more sentences with a number of words that have motivational or spiritual value. Because of their length, people cannot easily remember them. They write the words down and frequently repeat them only to find that they still did not precisely memorize them. For some this may be a reason to abandon the practice, others find it takes too long to master. The AHA method is so simple that there is hardly any time involved, just seven seconds—that's all.

An AHA consists of just three words put together into a meaningful phrase. The power of only three words can be tremendous. Just realize how major companies use them as highly successful slogans in promoting attention for a product. Examples are:

- Nike: *Just Do It*
- Sony: *like.no.other*
- Life is good: *Life is good*
- Philips: *Sense and Simplicity*
- Adidas: *Impossible is Nothing*
- General Electric: *Imagination at Work*

Here we come to the point where once again, *it's not what you think.* Taking an AHA and simply saying it a few times may not give you the desired result. That is because you need to do something else first to make this method automatic, so really something you do by feel, without thinking. As promised, you will only need a total of seven seconds for the complete sequence.

The AHA Method

The AHA method is in fact a simplified, yet very effective, form of self-hypnosis. As described in chapter two, in all forms of hypnotic induction it is important to bypass the *gatekeeper*, so that selective suggestions can be installed in the subconscious mind. This part of the mind has been called *the most powerful goal-achieving agency known to man*. It means that each program that is installed becomes part of the *autopilot* of the mind and will become active when properly triggered. When the new program is running, you have to follow it.

The more meaningful the suggestions are and the more frequent the message is compounded, the stronger the effect. Therefore, people go for their initial programming to a hypnosis specialist. Similar to creating physical strength with the help of a trainer, a hypnosis practitioner can be seen as a *personal coach* for the mind. When creating a state of hypnosis, these three key elements appear to always be involved:

1. Activating imagination
2. Healing breath
3. Applying suggestion

Activating imagination

This starts when you focus on your inner vision. You find this in your brow chakra (third eye) and the best way to begin is by closing your eyelids. By disconnecting from your outer visual perception you can concentrate easily on your inner perception. From there you can guide your thoughts into feelings. Imagination is sometimes called fantasy, make-believe, or visualization. Whatever name you use, make sure there is a sense of relaxation behind it— so no pressure.

Healing breath

This occurs when you deliberately allow your lungs to inhale. With the airflow you allow inspiration (this is the same as breathing in) to enter. The lungs can expand because the inhalation muscles receive a message from your mind. There are seven minor muscle groups involved but the two most important ones are the external intercostal muscles and the diaphragm in your midriff. The diaphragm, especially, is the one to pay extra attention to. Using this muscle creates belly breathing, which energizes the third chakra (solar plexus) and soothes the internal organs.

Just taking three long, deep breaths like this can already significantly regulate your heart rate, blood pressure, and stress levels.

Applying suggestion

Will make this into a hypnotic method. There are two ways in which your preferred AHA can be installed— through an external source or an internal one. Someone can help you by repeating the phrases at least three times or you can record your phrase with your own voice first and then play it back.

The fastest way is to have your own inner voice say the AHA rapidly three times, each time increasing the (imaginary) volume. Saying the AHA out loud is fine when you are by yourself, but may not work in public or social circumstances.

The Seven-Word Technique

Hypnosis can be explained as *meditation with a target*, so while practicing your technique, make sure you write your AHA of choice on a piece of paper and read it out loud at least three times. In this way, it will echo on while you are training your mind so you become highly focused on your intent. You may first want to use a general AHA such as *I am happy* and shift to different ones later.

This is an example of a seven-second AHA method:

1. Eyes closed
2. Deep breath
3. *I am happy*

Notice how there are exactly seven words in this method and from start to finish it takes only seven seconds to follow these instructions. The words of step three are the only ones that you change, depending on your personal situation. Below is a reference list to make targeting your intent easy. Of course, you can always make up your own AHA but make sure it stays within the boundaries of positivity. In other words, avoid the words *not*, *don't*, or any other words with a negative connotation.

AHA Reference List

When you look at the list of seventy-seven AHAs below, you will notice that some of them are grouped in trios that each start with the same word for easy reference. Then there are single AHAs that have a unique quality. Some of them may be more appealing to you because they apply more to your circumstances than others. I would like to encourage you to add your own AHAs or ask people close to you for advice.

Ask them what three-word phrase they can come up with to help you get into an instantaneous happy mood. Most people will jump to that opportunity because your positivity would rub off on them. Creating joy is a fun thing to do, especially with children. The AHA method is profound but simple enough for kids to learn and use in everyday situations.

Just imagine how your life can positively change when you use this seven-second method in situations like these:

- You don't feel hungry but you can't stop eating.
- You want to sleep but the harder you try the more awake you are.
- Your flight is ready to take off and you feel beyond uncomfortable.
- You're trying to be creative but you have no inspiration whatsoever.
- You're losing your self-control during an argument with a loved one.
- You are doing an exam and your nerves prevent you from concentrating.
- You're at the dentist for a treatment and your anxiety level is off the charts.

AHA Reference List

All is well
All things pass
All will resolve
Change that belief
Change my attitude
Change this feeling
Do it now
Do your best
Do something nice
I am good
I am ready
I am happy
I feel OK
I love you
I will survive
Just do it
Just let go
Just have fun
Let it be
Let love rule
Let peace come
Life is great
Life goes on
Life will prevail
Lift me up
Lift the veil
Lift this heaviness
Now I heal
Now I begin
Now things improve
Oh, I understand
Oh, my goodness
Oh, how wonderful
Pull it off
Pull me through
Pull yourself together
Shift to positivity
Shift happens easily
Shift my consciousness
Show your smile
Show true emotion

Show some courage
Take it easy
Take charge now
Take action immediately
Thanks a lot
Thanks for that
Thanks so much
Things get better
Things shall pass
Things are improving
This feels good
This is relaxing
This makes sense
Time will tell
Time can heal
Time is precious
Use your mind
Use what works
Use good judgment
Work it out
Work that body
Work with integrity
Yes I do
Yes I see
Yes I can

I am determined
Is that so?
Live with passion
Meditation brings peace
Money is energy
My income increases
My life improves
Patience is prudence
Time heals everything
We shall overcome

Your personal AHAs

. . . .

. . . .

The Three Cs

After an AHA moment, most people experience a feeling of either one (or all) of the three Cs: *Calmness, Clarity, and Confidence.*

Calmness

This is the mental state of being free from agitation, excitement, or disturbance. Calmness is a quality that can be cultivated and increased with practice. It takes a trained mind to stay calm in the face of a great deal of different stimulation, and possible distractions, especially emotional ones.

Clarity

This is a state of mind where you have clearness or lucidity of understanding, freedom from indistinctness or ambiguity. Often, a sudden flash of insight (aha!) will put you in this state of enlightenment.

Confidence

This is a state of being certain either that something is correct or that a certain action is the best or most effective. Confidence can be a self-fulfilling prophecy. If you don't have it, for instance because of bad experiences, you may fail or not try. If you do have it, you can become tremendously successful even without special abilities.

The three Cs could be used as an AHA in itself and from there your mood can move in a continuous upward spiral, especially if you keep compounding the message. In real life this is a method that actually works, because it is short and sweet and readily available. No devices or gadgets are required, all you need is a flash of insight so that you can shift your mind in the direction you want it to go, as long as you *tap the app* (there's another AHA for you).

Man seems to have made the computer in his own image, with working memory and storage capacity. Therefore, computer language works well to describe how the human mind processes information. Programming the mind is like programming a computer and downloading applications may take some initial patience, but once it's installed all it needs is regular updates.

Our habits are like programs that are created through *coded information,* gradually written and refined over time. Decoding the healing power of the mind is an important part of my work as a healer. Simplifying the process so people can learn how to be calm, clear, and confident in any situation is part of my mission.

Simplifying Complexity

As you move through life you are likely to run into challenges that can lead to a complexity of problems. At one point you may come to the conclusion that you have become lost in a labyrinth or stuck in a web with no way to escape. That usually is a good time to ask for help. The decision to heal the complexity of your life is always your own individual responsibility. The Law of Attraction applies, but there is no secret to it— when you ask for help, *help will arrive* (as the AHA goes).

Creating awareness of your problems and then allowing yourself to get into the right mindset is the first stage of your process of transformation. Ultimately, you would like to fully embrace your new identity and move from who you *used to be* to whom you *choose to be.* While you are on this journey you can feel happy despite the fact that you have not yet graduated from your new training course in life.

Over the past twenty-five years, many of my clients have begun to regard me as a healing mentor or coach guiding them through the many stages of healing. Some of them initially needed acute and life-saving care, others decided to embark on a quest to find more meaning and joy and get to know their true potential in this lifetime. With all of them I have used a combination of the variety of healing modalities I have described in this book. The range of techniques and methods can apply to anyone's situation but not always at the same time.

That's why people go to a healer like me who can use his intuitive capacity to simplify and speed up the process. Whether the complexity of your life revolves around physical, emotional, mental or spiritual challenges, healing is always possible. You may think you know what you problem is and how to solve it, but very often *it's not what you think.*

Finding healing solutions is complex enough by itself and for someone unfamiliar with the overwhelming amount of possibilities, it can become mind boggling instead of mind opening.

Gratitude

I hope this book has opened your mind to the concept of energy healing and created more clarity about the various ways in which healing can happen. I am thankful that you have honored my work with your attention. In essence, we are all energy and our gratitude determines our attitude.

I believe that happiness and healing are states of the mind and body we can promote by focusing on what is positive and conducting what is light. If this book has in some way positively enlightened you, I am tremendously grateful. My wish is that all people will learn to reflect positive energy onto others and contribute to creating a peaceful, happy world.

APPENDIX

INNER HEALING SERIES
SELF-HELP RESOURCES

These audio CDs have been designed by Marcel and Dr. Sonja to support you in your healing process. They can help you connect with and activate your powerful Inner Healing Force. The CDs are not intended to be a replacement of medical care. Always consult with your health care practitioner first if you are experiencing health problems.

Deep Relaxation
A 20-minute vacation to either a tropical beach or a peaceful forest allowing your body and mind to deeply relax.

Protected By The Light
Creative imagery to help improve the immune system and to aid in the recovery from illness. Use the power of the mind to help heal the body.

Magical Weight Loss
Helps you to achieve and maintain normal weight. This innovative and empowering program teaches you effective and life-changing ways to help you visualize and achieve your ideal weight.

Freedom From Pain
Two self-help methods to release and manage chronic pain. Learn to use your mind to reduce and eliminate persistent pain and discomfort.

Freedom From Stress
Guided imagery to help you automatically relax into stressful situations. Guides you to release stress and tension. Gain confidence, handle stressful situations better and live a happier, more productive life.

You Can Heal
Become an active participant in your healing process. Appeal to the power of your Higher Self to help you heal. Helps you to get in touch with the emotional issues of disease and to release them.

Medical Intuition
Learn how to use your intuition to discover a pathway to healing. Connect with your inner guide to find the cause of your personal problem or disease and how to heal it.

Healing Through Forgiveness
Forgiveness is a powerful healer. Guides you to heal through the process of forgiving and releasing negative emotions. Regain your personal power.

Rest & Relaxation
Escape to tranquility and allow this 20-minute mini vacation to a tropical beach help you relax deeply and leave your worries behind.

The Powerful Mind
Explains how the mind works and how it affects healing. You will also learn three fast and effective self-hypnosis techniques.

Chakra Hypnosis
A guided trance to help scan heal and balance your subtle energy centers and recharge your body's major systems.

Meditation Music For Someone Special
This healing music takes you to a deeply relaxed state and inspires realms of meditation, higher consciousness and healing. Three 20-minute compositions with morning, afternoon and evening vibrations. Ideal music for meditation, healing and relaxation.

Daydreams

On this popular instrumental album, guitar duets mixed with healing sounds are used to help you relax deeply, meditate and facilitate healing. The soothing, calming guitar music helps you to transcend time and release your tensions and stresses. Ideal background music for various healing purposes.

Happy Songs For Healing and Joy

Joyful music with optimistic and uplifting lyrics, combined with guided imagery, affirmations and prayer to bring back the joy of living and speed up the healing process. A magical CD suitable for kids as well as grown-ups to heal their inner child.

Soulmates

A selection of original songs from the heart that inspire, motivate and encourage you on your life's path. Let the music and lyrics move you from individual and relationship challenges to meaningful connections and the fulfillment of your life's purpose.

Order Inner Healing Series CDs at

www.consultmarcel.com

www.askforgoodhealth.com

Recommended Reading

Adams, Marilee, *Change Your Questions, Change Your Life*, Berrett-Koehler Publishers, 2009

Banyan, Calvin D. & Kein, Gerald F., *Hypnosis and Hypnotherapy*, Abbot Publishing House, 2001

Bolduc, Henry l., *Your Creative Voice*, Adventures Into Time Publishers, 1996

Bradford, Michael, *The Healing Energy of Your Hands*, The Crossing Press, 1995

Burchard, Brendon, *The Millionaire Messenger*, Morgan James Publishing, 2011

Chopra, Deepak, MD, *Quantum Healing*, Bantam Books, 1989

Covey, Stephen R., *The 7 Habits of Highly Effective People*, Fireside, 1990

De Graaff van Mastrigt, Sonja, *The Effects of Guided Imagery on White Blood Cell Count*, Greenwich University, 2001

Dossey, Larry, MD, *Healing Words*, Harper Collins, 1993

Elman, Dave, *Hypnotherapy*, Westwood Publishing, 1964

Epstein, Donald M. & Alman, Nathaniel, *The 12 Stages of Healing*, Amber-Allen Publishing, 1994

Gaynor, Mitchell L., MD, *Sounds of Healing*, Broadway Books, 1999

Gray, John, PhD, *How to Get What You Want and Want What You Have*, Harper Collins, 1999

Hay, Louise L., *You Can Heal Your Life*, Hay House, 1984

HH Dalai Lama & Cutler, Howard C., MD, *The Art of Happiness*, Riverhead Books, 1998

Jourdain, Robert, *Music, the Brain and Ecstacy*, Avon Books, 1997

Lipton, Bruce H., PhD, *The Biology of Belief*, Hay House, 2008

Loyd, Alex, PhD, ND & Ben Johnson, MD, DO, NMD, *The Healing Code*, Intermedia Publishing Group, 2010

Myss, Caroline, *Anatomy of the Spirit*, Crown Publishers, 1996

Nhat Hahn, Thich, *Peace Is Every Step*, Bantam Books, 1991

Nicoli, Thomas, *Thinking Thin— The Truth about Weight Loss*, Kalisti Publishing, 2007

Parkhill, Stephen, *Answer Cancer*, Health Communications, 1995

Peale, Norman Vincent, *The Power of Positive Thinking*, Ballantine Books, 1996

Perry, Wayne, *Overtoning*, Musikarma Publishing, 2005

Pert, Candace B., PhD, *Molecules of Emotions*, Simon & Schuster, 1999

Robbins, Anthony, *Unlimited Power*, Ballantine Books, 1986

Rothman, Stephanie (editor), *Everyday Miracles of Hypnotherapy*, BookSurge, 2004

Ruiz, Don Miguel, MD, *The Four Agreements*, Amber-Allen Publishing, 1997

Siegel, Bernie S. MD, *Love, Medicine & Miracles*, Harper & Row Publishers, 1986

Stearn, Jesse, *Edgar Cayce, The Sleeping Prophet*, Bantam Books, 1989

Sutphen, Dick & Tara, *Soul Agreements*, Hampton Roads Publishing, 2005

Tolle, Eckhart, *The Power of Now*, Namaste Publishing, 1997

Weil Andrew, MD, *Spontaneous Healing*, Alfred A. Knopf, 1995

Young-Sowers, Meredith, L., *Wisdom Bowls*, Stillpoint Publishing, 2002

About The Author

Marcel has been blessed with an extraordinary gift of helping people heal with energy frequencies. He combines this gift with his skills and training in mind power, sound healing and motivational coaching. Marcel has devoted his life to helping people heal with his unique abilities.

Marcel has helped thousands of clients from all walks of life overcome complex physical, emotional and behavioral challenges. His unique healing methods provide a practical framework to facilitate instant positive change, creating rapid and long-lasting results.

Marcel has appeared on various media programs and he is a well-respected member of the professional healing community. He is an active volunteer for several non-profit organizations, as well as specialty care children's hospitals. His advocates include teachers, parents, physicians, psychologists, politicians, celebrities and members of royal families.

A talented musician since childhood, Marcel also uses the essence of vibrational healing in his music compositions. His popular music albums serve as an ideal tool for healing. Marcel is the producer of audio CDs that promote healing and self-improvement through imagery, sound and music. He is co-author of the book *Everyday Miracles in Hypnotherapy*.

An in-demand public speaker, dynamic seminar presenter and respected adjunct faculty member of the National Guild of Hypnotists (NGH), Marcel is an internationally recognized board certified hypnosis specialist. More than two decades of experience in private practice have given him a reputation of excellence.

Made in the USA
Charleston, SC
29 July 2012